The Wedding
by
Peter Lacey

A
Ridge Press Book
☀
Madison Square Press
Grosset & Dunlap
New York

The Wedding

by

Peter Lacey

Editor-in-Chief: Jerry Mason
Editor: Adolph Suehsdorf
Art Director: Albert Squillace
Associate Editor: Moira Duggan
Associate Editor: Barbara Hoffbeck
Art Associate: David Namias
Art Associate: Egbert Teague
Art Production: Doris Mullane

For Sheila

Contents

The time approach'd, to church the parties went,

At once with carnal and devout intent:

Forth came the priest, and bade th' obedient wife,

Like Sarah, or Rebecca, lead her life:

Then pray'd the pow'rs the fruitful bed to bless,

And made all sure enough with holiness.

The Merchant's Tale, THE CANTERBURY TALES

Part I. The Wedding

Since Time Began

Glories of the Wedding

*Preceding pages:
Flemish wedding
procession by
the Elder Brueghel has
groom (between trees,
left) leading men
and complacent bride
(right, center)
escorted by women.
Opposite: Late
13th-century miniature
of Adam and Eve,
the first couple.*

ur world is encompassed by the sounds and scenes of weddings. Bells ring, incense burns, choirs sing, priests pray, magicians chant spells, clerks pronounce the sanction of the state, vows are exchanged, mothers weep, rice is thrown, wine drunk, tea sipped, cake eaten, wedding dances are danced—and men and women are united in marriage. Like birth and death, this universal nuptial symphony is ceaseless.

The origin of the wedding lies too far in the past to be traced. As a ceremony it has been known and celebrated in all societies at all times. It is a fundamental experience in the life of mankind, formalizing the partnership of male and female and the family as an institution.

It has evolved in myriad forms, each elaborated with rites, symbols, and customs. Many early wedding customs have survived to our time, although we may have no knowledge of their original purpose and meaning. The wedding vows, prayers, and oaths of most religions and societies are usually quite explicit ("to have and to hold," "honor and obey"), but the embellishments are not.

Why, for instance, do we have wedding rings, bridal veils, special cakes, and wedding dances? Why that special metal for the wedding ring, this particular blossom for the bride to carry, that specific color for her dress?

To find some of the answers we might look to a time when men and women were less estranged from their nature and purpose than they so often are today: the age of the Elizabethans. These English men and women of the late sixteenth and early seventeenth centuries were a stimulating blend of modern thinkers and superstitious traditionalists. And they loved weddings. Robert Herrick expressed their enthusiasm:

> *"Next we will act how young men wooe;*
> *And sigh, and kisse, as lovers do,*
> *And talk of brides, and who shall make*
> *That wedding-smock, this bridal-cake;*
> *That dress, this sprig, that leafe, this vine;*
> *That smooth and silken columbine.*
> *This done, we'll draw lots, who shall buy*
> *And guild the bayes and rosemary:*
> *What posies for our wedding-rings;*
> *What gloves we'll give and ribbanings."*

The livelier the wedding, the better. The more lavish and pretentious, the better. The more wine or ale to drink, the better. For it was to pleasure that the Elizabethans—bride, groom, families, guests, onlookers—dedicated themselves at a wedding. The times were right for joy. Man was obviously entering an era of power and attainment. Life seemed new and bold, yet the old was valued, too. Ancient wedding customs were revered and occasionally revived by the Elizabethans. The traditions that continue in American weddings are largely those preserved by Elizabethan custom.

Like most people before the twentieth century, the Elizabethans had to furnish almost all of their own entertainment. They had theaters in the city, traveling players and buffoons, the pomp and pageantry of royal visits and events, but these diversions were only occasional. And so weddings ranked high as entertainment. They offered spectacle and significance, and were always followed by a celebration which included drinking, feasting, dancing, music, and general enjoyment.

True, the noise and ostentation of these proceedings prompted criticism by Puritan divines and some of the soberer Anglican bishops. But they stormed in vain. Censure could not subdue, nor invective stifle, the Renaissance Englishman's love for nuptial festivities.

Rank and wealth, as always, dictated the terms of observance and celebration. But in every case the people involved followed what they thought to be the essential practices and pleasures. Since marriage was necessary for the preservation and protection of the all-important family and since divorce was extremely difficult, they knew the marriage was forever.

The early Elizabethan wedding was usually arranged, especially among the middle class and the nobility. Marriage was too important an affair to be left to chancy love; that might develop after the wedding.

Romantic love was present, though, as it has been throughout time. Shakespeare's plays and sonnets, Herrick's poems, and lockets painted with lovers' portraits testify to its existence. And, though still a lesser factor in the usual wedding arrangements, love was beginning to win converts. Queen Elizabeth's tutor, Roger Ascham, wrote, "Our time is so far from that old discipline and obedience as now, not only young gentlemen, but even very young girls dare without all fear though not without open shame,

Satirical spirit
pervades Brueghel
painting of
bridal procession.
Plump bride behind
pipes has air
of smug sanctity,
but Brueghel's
contemporaries knew
that facts of peasant
life were earthier.

where they list and how they list marry themselves in spite of father, mother, God, good order, and all." That last "and all" has a rather desperate sound to it; indeed, the age of the love marriage was beginning.

Rank and fortune still came first, however. The Elizabethan family was much concerned with preserving and enlarging its wealth, power, and social standing, and the choice of a marriage partner was often made with advancement in mind. Once a match had been agreed upon between families, a marriage contract was drawn up and a chaperoned courtship of the prospective bride by her fiancée began its brief course. As the families and their intermediaries argued the marriage settlement, the betrothed couple dallied, danced, and discoursed, exchanged gifts and flattery, and steadily appraised each other. Finally, a contract being agreed upon and signed, a date was set for the nuptials.

Certain months were favored for weddings, April and November particularly. Morning was the most popular time of day, because of an old custom that dictated marriage before noon. Thus, the early hours of the appointed day were a time of busy preparation for the wedding ceremony and celebration.

Before the bride awoke the servants prepared the house. Some had been up all night scrubbing, dusting, and cooking. Others were aroused at dawn. Sweet scent and beauty must pervade the house, so rosemary and roses were strewn in all the rooms and corridors, forming a soft carpet of blossoms.

After the bride awakened, the two chief bridesmaids began their morning's task of dressing her. The bride herself probably had chosen her bridal gown. It was carefully designed and sewn from a fabric which was usually white, for innocence, and of the finest possible texture: cloth of gold for the nobility, perhaps cloth of silver for others, or white silk or linen homespun—the best that her family could afford.

The other bridesmaids tied "love knots" of colored ribbons which were to be sewed on the bodice, sleeves, and skirt of the wedding gown. The knots symbolized the wedding tie, and their colors could be variously interpreted. Some might mean virtue and good fortune, others vice. Green, for instance, would be worn by brides who thought it signified fidelity and shunned by those who believed it meant wantonness.

When the bride's ribbons were tied, three essential ornaments were added to her costume: her engagement ring, which probably had not been removed from the day it was put on; the "brooch of innocence" to be worn on her breast; and the bouquet, or garland, of blossoms which she would carry or wear through the wedding ceremony.

The garland—a tribute to and symbol of the bride's virtue—could also be worn on her head. The flowers of the garland (rosemary—"for remembrance"—was a favorite) often were gilded. The veil that completed the bride's costume could be her own hair, combed and brushed to hang straight or braided down her back. A royal bride of the time was more elaborately dressed. When Princess Elizabeth, the daughter of King James I, married Frederick, the Elector of Bohemia, in 1613, a contemporary observer wrote that "Her vestements were white, the emblem of innocency; her hair dishevelled, hanging down her back at length, an ornament of virginity; a crown of pure gold upon her head the cognizance of majesty...her train supported by twelve young ladies in white garments, so adorned with jewels, that her passage looked like a milky way."

There was still much for the bridesmaids to do before the ceremony began. They had to knot yards of rope with fresh flowers for hanging throughout the house. They supervised the strewing of a path of soft rushes and roses between the bride's house and the church. And they had to make dozens of little "favor" bouquets for themselves to wear and the guests to carry.

Meanwhile, at the groom's house, his men were busy adorning him with rosettes and ribbon streamers in the colors chosen by the bride. They also trimmed his beard and hair. Indeed, the groom looked almost as splendid as the bride; Elizabethan male finery had yet to be sombered by Puritan plainness.

For their hectic, careful work these bridesmaids and grooms-men were given special tokens of thanks by the bride and groom: silk scarves for the maids, fine gloves for the men. Even the wedding guests received gift rings commemorating the wedding.

By ten o'clock in the morning, wedding work in the bride's home had to be near completion. Very soon the sounds of flutes, horns, drums, and cymbals would be dinning at the door to summon the bride and her attendants. With the minstrel band were the groomsmen, come to escort the bridal party to the church where the groom awaited them. This procession was one of the high points of any Elizabethan wedding. Onlookers re-garded it as excellent entertainment and were likely to join it if not discouraged from doing so by the groomsmen.

Conscious of their performance and wonderfully colorful in their finery, the members of the bridal party assembled within the door before stepping out onto the rush-strewn path. First came the musicians, then a flower bearer with a silver gilt "bride's cup," beribboned with the bridal colors and containing a gilded rosemary branch. Next came the bride herself between two pages or bachelors, followed by her bridesmaids. Some of the brides-maids bore bridecakes for the guests; others carried gilded wheat sheaves. Both the cakes and sheaves were symbolic of hoped-for fertility in the new marriage. Last came the parents, relatives,

friends, and guests, all of them dressed in their finest clothes and probably beribboned as well.

Preceded by the musicians and a little girl carrying a flower basket and a little boy bearing the wedding ring on a cushion, the bridal party filed into the church and up to the altar. The presence of children at the head of the procession also was thought to encourage fertility, a reminder of marriage's purpose. The guests meanwhile took their places.

At the altar the groom stood with the bride at his left side as the minister or church official began the ceremony, reciting the

Brueghel's groom, wearing red hat and crown, is accompanied to church by rustic friends and musician playing pipe and tabor.

21

wedding service from the English Prayer Book:

"Dearly beloved, we are gathered here in the sight of God, and in the face of this company, to join together this Man and this Woman in holy Matrimony; which is an honorable estate instituted of God in the time of man's innocency, signifying unto us this mystical union that is betwixt God and his Church."

Pausing to ask if there were any objections to the nuptials, the minister then proceeded to the *de futuro* vows in which the couple promised to love, comfort, honor, and obey. Next came the *de praesenti* vows which formed the core of the wedding ceremony. Taking the bride's ungloved right hand in his own right hand, the groom repeated after the minister: "I take thee to be my wedded Wife, to have and to hold from this day forward, for better and for worse, for richer and for poorer, in sickness and in health, to love and to cherish, till death do us part, according to God's ordinance, and thereto I plight thee my troth."

In her turn, the bride took the groom's hand in hers and also repeated after the minister: "I take thee to be my Husband, to have and to hold from this day forward, for better and for worse, for richer and for poorer, in sickness and in health, to love, cherish, and to obey, till death do us part, according to God's ordinance; and thereto I give thee my troth."

Following these vows, the wedding ring was put on. It might be elaborate or plain; one popular style was made up of three circlets joined together, each circlet containing one line of a verse. The groom placed the ring on the bride's finger while saying, "With this ring I thee wed, and with all my worldly goods I thee endow; in the name of the Father, and of the Son, and of the Holy Ghost. Amen." All of the history and mystic power of the marriage seemed to be embodied in the symbolic circlet.

As the couple knelt at the altar beneath a canopy held by four ecclesiastics, the minister pronounced them man and wife with this benediction: "God the Father, God the Son, and God the Holy Ghost, bless, preserve, and keep you; the Lord mercifully with his favor look upon you, and fill you with all spiritual benediction and grace; that ye may so live together in this life, that in the world to come ye may have life everlasting. Amen."

There followed, inevitably, a sermon on marriage with references to appropriate passages in the Scriptures. These sermons were popular and the better ones often were widely discussed and even printed.

The sermon over, the famished wedding party rose as one and eagerly pressed to the front of the church. There wine and the bridecake were served to fortify them for the procession back to the bride's home. The bridecup, filled with wine and the rosemary sprig, was passed from hand to hand.

There was also much happy kissing. In earlier weddings, the priest had given a "benediction kiss" to the groom which the groom in turn passed along to the bride; the priest's assistants had then solemnly kissed each of the wedding guests. Now, although the minister still kissed the groom, the guests did their own kissing. The sanctity of the church was remembered at most weddings, however, and decorum was preserved.

The wedding party now returned to the bride's home. As before, the musicians accompanied them. On the way, perhaps, the bride and groom might be compelled to jump over a stone or flower garland. If they refused, the bride might be kissed by as many men as could pull her from the two married men escorting her from the church.

When she finally reached the house, the bride probably paused for a moment before entering the door. She knew that just beyond it there were bridesmaids and guests waiting to break small

"Peasant Dance" by Younger Brueghel celebrates wedding of bride in background, again wreathed and sitting under crown. Her plate holds gift of coins.

cakes over her head and the groom's. These little cakes, made of eggs, milk, sugar, spice, and currants, had a special importance at every wedding. They were superstitiously saved by some of the guests and placed under their pillows to bring pleasant dreams. Others passed the pieces of cake through their wedding rings before throwing them at the newlyweds as they ran through the door. Still others, believing that the presence of these broken cakes would help ease the defloration of the bride, scattered cake crumbs on the wedding bed. What cakes the guests left were stacked before the new couple during the wedding feast.

As the celebration began, the guests inspected the displayed wedding presents, which might include household linens, candle-sticks, silverware, warming pans, cookware, fireplace sets, and draperies or tapestries, even money. All weddings were important events and people gave generously to the new couple.

The feast and merriment probably lasted two or three days, though longer wedding festivities were common, especially among the rich who might provide masques, plays, pageants, or games for the guests' entertainment. The feasting itself, with as much good food as could be provided by host and guests alike, was washed down by huge quantities of wine or ale. The neighborhood poor, on the fringes of the celebration, were also given food and drink as long as the festivities lasted.

After the eating, the dancing began. Men and women leapt and danced, skirts flew, and ribbons fluttered in the air. One spoilsport complained: "Some cannot be merry without a noise of fiddlers, who scrape acquaintance at the first sight; nor sing, unless the divell himself come in for a part, and the ditty be made in hell." But few paid him any heed.

As the evening grew later, the noise grew louder, the dancing more frenetic, the songs more bawdy, and the new couple more sleepy. Yet the bride and groom had to stay up as late as possible and then be ushered to the bridal chamber with pomp and ceremony.

When the bride let it be known that she was ready for bed, the groomsmen and other guests attempted to untie the knotted ribbons on her gown. Untying these knots would supposedly insure easy childbirth for her. The bride also took off her slippers, gloves, and garters as gifts for the groomsmen. At last, rescued by her bridesmaids, she was taken to the bridal chamber and dressed for bed. Joined by the bridegroom in the bed, she might sit sedately, receiving guests and saying goodnight. Then the new couple was finally left alone amidst the crumbs of the bridecake. In the morning the two would be awakened by music being played beneath their window.

Antiquity: Fertility and Abundance

nnually, in the spring, a Catholic priest leaves the ancient Peruvian city of Cuzco and makes his way high up into the Andes mountains. He brings with him his holy vestments and a Bible, for the purpose of his journey is to conduct a group marriage ceremony and to baptize babies. It is customary to do this each year, and has been for centuries.

Awaiting the priest patiently in a high valley are a score or so of men and women. These couples have with them their children and llamas. The men have the proud faces of Inca warriors and are cloaked in colorful blankets. The women, incongruously, wear derbies on their fine Indian heads and long cotton dresses under their woolen shawls. Some couples are there to have their newborn children baptized, some are there to be married, and some are there for both reasons.

These are the highest-dwelling of the Peruvian Catholics and they are too remote, too poor to have their own priests. But the church recognizes the hardship of life for these people and it also knows their ancient customs. It consecrates the marriages they have made themselves and baptizes the children of these unions. So the new couples remain Catholic in their special Incan way and everyone is made happy by the wedding.

It may not be a simple coincidence that there were similar mass weddings in the area during the days of the Incan empire, which came to its abrupt and bloody end four centuries ago. Then, it was the Emperor of the Incas himself who performed the ceremony, and the ritual had an additional significance. It was believed that the uniting of the brides and grooms was related to the crucial uniting of the sky and earth that produced crops.

The Incan marriage fertility ceremony was not unique among peoples. In fact, it was typical of many similar rites practiced by prehistoric and primitive societies. These rituals had the same general purpose: to propitiate the gods of life. Fertility, abundance, and good fortune were the sought-for results. Today the memory of this ancient, purposeful magic lingers on in the wedding folklore and superstitions of many societies, including our own. Our wedding customs are thus important relics of man's prehistoric beliefs and rites.

The origin of the wedding ceremony is naturally a subject of conjecture and debate. No one can be sure when and why it actually began. Some believe that marriage is rooted in economic necessity, in the taking of a wife as an economic asset. At least one historian has believed that marriage began as a form of slavery; a wedding ceremony in this view has something of the status of a legal procedure. Other reasons offered for the origin of marriage have been sexual desire, social companionship, or the care of children; here the wedding is seen as a personal or social contract. In different societies marriage might exist for a single such reason or for a combination of them. What is certain is that all known human societies have had some form of ceremonial marriage, and that monogamy—one wife for one husband—seems to be the rule, not the exception. (Other forms of marriage, such as polygamy—more than one wife, and polyandry—more than one husband, seem to be special social answers to biological or economic necessities.) Regardless of the reasons for marriage and its forms, there seems almost always to have been a ceremony— a wedding—of some kind to solemnize and mark the new union. The word "wedding" itself comes from "wedd," the Anglo-Saxon word meaning pledge.

The supernatural significance that primitive man attached to the wedding ceremony can be easily understood when we recall how much early man was subject to the forces of nature and to his own ignorance. Life depended on the abundance of the game that he hunted and the fertility of the plants he harvested. It was perhaps inevitable that man in his ignorance would attempt to magically invoke the abundance, fertility, and protection he needed for survival. One such form of magic was the ritual wedding, in which the symbolic and actual union of a man and a woman echoed the mysterious life-force itself.

Originally, it seems, these ritual weddings involved the shedding of blood, often in the form of human sacrifice. In his book, *The Greek Myths,* poet-scholar Robert Graves has offered his ideas about the meaning of these primitive marriage rituals of prehistory. One of the central practices of prehistoric Greek religion was, according to Graves, the magic-making marriage of a male member of a tribe to the tribal "goddess," or priestess. The priestess was believed to be the personification of the goddess of life itself. Her symbols were the sun and the moon, mainly the mysterious moon. As the earthly representative of the goddess, she yearly chose a sacred king from the winners of contests such

Kneeling father of Panamanian Indian bride of 17th century offers her dowry —bow and arrows—as preparations are made for celebration.

30

as foot races, archery, and wrestling. Their wedding was marked with great solemnity and for one year the now-sacred "king" reigned over the tribe as consort of the goddess. But at the end of his reign—in the bleakness of midwinter—he had to die, a sacrificial inducement to the goddess to renew life in the spring.

The original basis of this belief in a supreme goddess was, Graves believes, early man's ignorance of the connection between coition and birth; women were believed to be the apparently independent and myterious source of life. Eventually, however, men became aware of their own role in creation and would no longer submit to sacrifice. The temporary kings prolonged their reigns and, eventually, masculine power became dominant, both in Greece and elsewhere. Whereas in the prehistoric period family descent had been matrilineal—family names, property, and rights descending on the mother's side, rather than the father's—by the beginning of historical time these customs had been reversed in most societies in favor of men. A bride now assumed her husband's name, and children and property descended in his line.

The extant writing of ancient civilizations tell us that as man emerged from the period of unrecorded history he continued to celebrate ritual or magic weddings. The ceremonies he practiced— if not including human sacrifice—still expressed his desire to obtain the favors of fertility and abundance from the gods.

In Sumeria, for example, the gods of the temples had their nun-like concubines, girls who were ceremonially married to the deities and who brought their dowries with them into the temple enclosure. These brides mated ritually with the kings and priests who represented the gods on earth, a fact that caused Victorian scholars to regard them as prostitutes. There seems no doubt now, though, that in their own societies these women were looked upon as sacred and revered wives.

There is evidence that on ancient Cyprus the early Phoenician princes or kings of Paphos were regularly wed to living symbols of the goddess Aphrodite. The royal males assumed the sacred name of Adonis. The bride in such a marriage, although she was the embodiment of the great goddess of prehistoric times, was nevertheless dominated by her male partner.

In ancient Athens there was an annual ceremony in which a chosen queen was married to a man representing the god of vegetation, Dionysus.

Marriages of gods or their images to human beings or objects continued to be performed, both to promote abundance and to avert such disasters as floods and disease. Symbols of the female earth and the male sky were married in tribal Africa and Egypt; in India and Germany fruit-bearing trees were ritually "married" in fertility ceremonies.

As recently as the nineteenth century the irrigation of the fields adjoining the Nile was helped by the "marriage" of an earthen "bride" to the river. The image was placed before the rising tide of the river and soon washed down. (Arab historians record that Moslem conquerors arriving in the area in the early Middle Ages found the inhabitants still in the practice of using living girls for river sacrifice rather than earthen images. The Moslems soon put a stop to the fatal ceremony, but similar bridal sacrifices to river gods were offered by an East African tribe as late as a hundred years ago.)

In Java a "rice-bride" and "rice-groom," each consisting of several ears of rice tied together, were ritually married before the harvest was begun. The new couple was even given a special bridal chamber in a corner of a barn and other sheaves of rice were placed around them to represent wedding guests. That the Javanese took the nuptials seriously is indicated by the fact that no one could go into the bridal barn for forty days for fear of disturbing the new couple. In northwestern India a similar marriage was made with two wooden dolls representing the rain gods. The wedding ceremony was performed in full on the day preceding the autumn sowing. When the rain began to fall the dolls were thrown into a stream.

In *The Golden Bough,* his monumental study of primitive religion, Sir James George Frazier convincingly traces the extension of the forms of the "sacred marriage" into modern wedding and folk customs—both civilized and uncivilized. For example, ritual intercourse—practiced at spring festivals by such diverse groups as the Peruvians, Javanese, and West Africans—occurred in more modest form in such European areas as the Ukraine. There, on St. George's Day (the 23rd of April) "young married people lie down in couples on the sown fields and roll several times over on them, in the belief that this will promote the growth of the crops."

Some of the German Whitsuntide celebrations were quite explicit about the fact that the spirit of the god of vegetation was the groom in their wedding pantomine. Others were more subtle.

In the region of Altmark, for instance, the villagers on Whitsuntide morning watched their children parade in a May Bride ceremony. The bride herself—a beautiful child dressed as a bride and wearing a posy of flowers in her hair—went from house to house, escorted by her child bridesmaids. Past each door she sang a song which told the villagers that if they gave her gifts they would prosper, but if they did not the reverse would be true. Beside the bride and surrounded by young boys marched her "groom": either a May-tree borne aloft, or a boy covered with leaves and flowers.

Of the Whitsuntide and May Day "brides and grooms," the

purest European vestiges of sacred marriage between a man and a woman representing deities, Frazer explains: "They were performing a serious magical rite, designed to make the woods grow green, the fresh grass sprout, the corn shoot, and the flowers blow." And ". . . in the opinion of those who performed [the rites] the marriage of trees and plants could not be fertile without the real union of the human sexes."

These charming rituals—finally the play of children—are now seldom celebrated. The machine and mechanized society have surpassed crops and animals and weather in the minds of men. The wedding is no longer so closely associated with the rhythm of natural life. So the symbolism and celebration of nature in connection with the wedding have all but died. To ancient men and, until very recently, to primitive men the wedding that marked the union of a man and woman was symbolic of the creation of all life. That is no longer the case. Most of us now live in cities and societies divorced from the land and the eternal processes of nature that governed the minds and lives of our ancestors. In achieving this separation from nature we have deprived the wedding of much of its true meaning. It is only by recalling to mind the ancient beliefs that we can understand many of the wedding customs remaining to us.

Throughout prehistory, then, the wedding was a social event of great importance, intimately associated with the vital processes of nature. It was a religious ceremony, too, of direct concern to the gods and goddesses who ruled man and nature.

By the time of classical Greece and the beginnings of western civilization many ritual wedding celebrations had been reduced to mere pantomime; the weddings of ordinary men and women, however, continued to be explicitly close to the realities of the natural world.

Greece: Marriage As A Duty

From the brawling warriors of the Homeric age to the philosopher-soldiers of the Periclean age, the ancient Greeks bore marriage more as a duty than as a pleasure. By the time of Plato in the fifth century B.C., the taking of a wife had become for many men a regrettable, if necessary, burden. There were still memories of the prehistoric past, when the hand of a queen-goddess was the prize of a contest, but somehow the prize had come to seem less worth winning.

The historian Herodotus, writing at about Plato's time, quotes a popular tale about King Cleisthenes of Sicyon, who wished to marry his daughter to the best man in Greece. From all over the Greek world came eager suitors, bursting with strength and virtue. The wealthiest and handsomest of them all was Hippocleides, an Athenian. Cleisthenes kept the suitors with him for a full year, testing them, conversing with them, eating, drinking, and exercising with them. All the while he appraised their various qualities and by the year's end had decided that Hippocleides would be his son-in-law and heir. He kept the decision to himself, however, for he intended to announce it with suitable pomp on the last day of the trial year. Herodotus tells the rest of the tale in Book VI of *The Persian Wars*.

"When at length the day arrived which had been fixed for the espousals, and Cleisthenes had to speak out and declare his

Ancient Greek vase is decorated with mythological scene of courting men and women, although most Greek marriages were arranged without preliminaries.

choice, he first of all made a sacrifice of one hundred oxen, and held a banquet whereat he entertained all the suitors, and the whole people of Sicyon. After the feast was ended, the suitors vied with each other in music and in speaking on a given subject. Presently, as the drinking advanced, Hippocleides, who quite dumbfounded the rest, called aloud to the fluteplayer, and bade him strike up a dance; which the man did, and Hippocleides danced to it. And he fancied that he was dancing excellently well; but Cleisthenes, who was observing him, began to misdoubt the whole business. Then Hippocleides, after a pause, told an attendant to bring in a table; and when it was brought he mounted upon it and danced first of all some Laconian figures, then some Attic ones; after which he stood on his head upon the table, and began to toss his legs about. Cleisthenes, nothwithstanding that he now loathed Hippocleides for a son-in-law, by reason of his dancing and his shamelessness, still, as he wished to avoid an outbreak, had restrained himself during the first and likewise during the second dance; when, however, he saw him tossing his legs in the air, he could no longer contain himself, but cried out, 'Son of Tisander, you have danced your wife away!' 'What does Hippocleides care?' was the other's answer."

The astounded Cleisthenes promptly gave his daughter to the second suitor on his list and the rest departed. Such were the depths to which heroic kingship by trial had sunk in the eyes of the classical Greeks. No woman was really worth all that trouble. "Mistresses we keep for pleasure, concubines for daily attendance upon our persons, and wives to bear us legitimate children and be our housekeepers," said the orator Demosthenes. Physical love (Eros) was a passion Greek men connected with beautiful courtesans or beautiful boys, but not with their wives.

The average bride was an uneducated, unquestioning child

of about fifteen. From the time of her birth she had been raised in her father's house, leaving it only for religious festivals or special occasions, never for sheer pleasure. Probably she had never even seen the man to whom her father had betrothed her. The transition from childhood to wifehood was abrupt. The night before her wedding the Greek bride reluctantly put away her juvenile playthings. "Timareta, being about to be married, has consecrated to thee, O Artemis of the Marshes, her tambourines, and the ball she was so fond of, and her hairnet; her dolls, too, she has dedicated in a befitting manner, with her clothes—a virgin's offering to thee, O virgin Goddess." Such a prayer was said by many Greek girls on the eve of their marriage.

What did Greek husbands expect of such youthful brides? That they be effective mistresses of the household slaves, efficient managers of their homes, and, above all, that they be fertile bearers of male children, for to the ancient Greeks the most important single reason for marriage was the perpetuation of their family through the male line. A man's ancestors fared well in the netherworld so long as they were worshipped by the living male members of the family. A man married so that when he died his son would continue the ancestral rites. For a legitimate son, a legal mother was necessary. For that reason there was great social pressure on any man who remained a bachelor. In Athens only married men could be legislators or generals, and in Sparta confirmed bachelors were heavily fined.

The ideal Greek wife was a passive mate. Plutarch tells us that the Greeks of Elis erected a statue of the goddess Aphrodite and dedicated it to marriage. The statue was designed by the sculptor Phidias who posed the goddess with one of her shapely feet placed on the shell of a turtle. The meaning of this detail did not escape the Greeks: A virtuous wife would emulate the silent, practically immobile reptile. She would confine herself to the "shell" of her home.

Some writers have seen a discrepancy between the almost oriental subjection of Greek women in fifth-century B.C., and the comparative independence and spirit of the wives and girls of the Greece of 1200 B.C., as Homer described them. The difference, however, was more of degree than of substance. In the rough life of Homeric Greece a wife was not only a childbearer, she was a necessary and valued aide to her often-absent warrior husband. But early Greece was nevertheless a thoroughly masculine society and women were even then the subjects of men.

In the *Odyssey,* Homer tells how King Menelaus, conqueror of Troy, gave

> " . . . a wedding banquet, made
> Both for his blameless daughter and his son,
> And many guests. Her he must send away,
> Bride of that invincible child,
> Achilles. He betrothed her while in Troy,
> And gave his kindly word, and now the gods
> Fulfilled it by the marriage."

It is quite clear that Menelaus had given the girl to Achilles in a betrothal ceremony that took place far from the intended bride. Eight hundred years later it still was not necessary for a Greek girl to be present at her betrothal. Since her consent was not required and since, like most women, she was kept from public gatherings, she was in fact probably not present. The betrothal was a matter between the intended bride's father and the intended groom (or the groom's father if he were a minor).

In an actual betrothal ceremony of the fifth century B.C. the suitor (or his father) clasped hands with the father of the bride-to-be in the presence of witnesses. The father simply promised to offer his daughter in marriage with a specified dowry.

This form of betrothal, though not in writing, was binding. Ancient peoples like the Greeks had profound respect for a verbal, public oath. No man would lightly repudiate one. Moreover, the ceremony had religious overtones and probably was performed in front of an altar. The betrothal (*engyesis*) was almost a wedding ceremony in itself, and in Greek law a marriage began legally from the day the betrothal was performed. What we would call the wedding was the *ekdosis*, or giving away of the bride to the bridegroom, and the core of that ceremony was the actual transfer, or procession of the bride from her father's house to the house of her new husband. *Gamos* (consummation), hopefully resulting in a male child, was the main purpose of marriage and was performed in the groom's bedchamber.

Appropriately enough, the ancient Greek month of *Gamelion* (January) was the most popular time for weddings; the name Gamelion means "wedding month," and the period was considered sacred to Hera, goddess of marriage. Like their prehistoric an-

Marriages of the gods intrigued Renaissance painters. Here Bacchus and Ariadne are crowned by Venus in work by Tintoretto.

cestors, the classical Greeks preferred to marry in the winter at the time of a full moon.

Before her wedding the bride was expected to take a ritual bath in water that had been carried from a special fountain. (The procession of water-bearers was a popular theme of Greek painting.) In Athens both the bride and groom bathed in water from the spring of Kallachoran to insure the birth of children.

By the morning of the wedding the bride's house, as well as the groom's, was decorated with garlands of olive and laurel leaves, symbols of plenty and virtue. The ceremonies began with sacrifices to the gods of marriage and a feast. In Homeric times, this wedding feast, though situated in the house of the bride's father, was paid for by the groom, who had also compensated the father for his daughter. Homer speaks of young girls "sought for their beauty with gifts of oxen."

During the wedding banquet, the new couple shared a sesame cake in order to absorb its fertile essence. The bride wore her finest clothes and was veiled, a wreath crowning her head. Around her were her female attendants and a special woman functionary called the *nympheutria* who was to guide her through the intricacies of the ceremonies. After the dinner, gifts were presented to the bride, and preparations began for the high point of the wedding: the procession to the groom's house.

In Athens, this procession was led by a wagon bearing the bride and groom. The bride bore a sieve and a gridiron, symbols of her new domestic life. As the wagon bumped slowly over the cobbled streets, it was followed by torchbearers, musicians, relatives, and friends. The torches flared fitfully in the dark and the houses lining the way echoed the cheers of onlookers and the rhythmic music of flutes, lyres, and tambourines. There is an ancient Greek vase in an Athens museum which shows perhaps the earliest instance of a modern postceremonial custom: a departing bride and groom having an old shoe thrown at them.

Inside her new home, the bride was taken to the hearth by the groom and there she was showered with dates, nuts, figs, little coins, and other symbols of fertility and prosperity. The time soon came for the real purpose of the wedding, and from the hearth the couple went straight to the bridal chamber. Red sheets covered their bed—supposedly to ease the defloration of the bride. As the bedroom door was closed behind them a friend of the groom posted himself before it as a guard. The rest of the wedding party then noisily sang nuptial hymns to encourage the couple and to frighten off evil spirits. Some, if not most of these songs, were bawdy or at least explicitly sexual; no one could doubt what they celebrated. Some of the finest poetry that has survived the ancient Greeks are such wedding songs, or epithalamia. Oddly enough, the greatest were written by the schoolmistress Sappho to some of her former pupils. In such song poems—which became famous in the classical world—the poet of Lesbos often lamented the loss of a lover at the same time she celebrated the wedding.

> *"Thou happy bridegroom! Now has dawned*
> *That day of days supreme,*
> *When in thine arms thou'lt hold at last*
> *The maiden of thy dream."*

For all of their seeming one-sidedness, however, the marriages of ancient Greece were fairly stable. Love was not a disruptive element. Moreover, if a wife was divorced and returned to her father, her dowry had to be returned, too. Plutarch tells how Alcibiades, most prodigal of the Athenians, boldly kidnapped his neglected wife from the very courtroom where she was seeking a divorce from him. It wasn't that he loved her and could not live without her; he had already spent the dowry.

Rome: Exaltation of the Family

A Roman wedding was a serious, stately affair and, at least in the days of the Republic, the marriage was a permanent one. The wedding was not only the ceremonial joining in marriage of a man and woman, but also the initiation of the bride into the family of the groom.

The Romans exalted family. A man's or woman's legal rights and social opportunities were largely determined by the status of the family into which he or she was born. There was a wide gap between patricians, who enjoyed the privileges of citizenship, and plebeians, who did not. Only at the end of the Republic, shortly before Christ, were the groups permitted to intermarry.

Because class lines were so rigidly drawn, and because families clung carefully to their social status and fortunes, the rights and responsibilities of brides and grooms were specifically defined from the moment of betrothal by Roman law and custom. A formal betrothal *(sponsalia)*, though not a legal requirement, was almost always observed as an essential bit of social etiquette. The *sponsalia* was literally a promise by the bride, or her father or guard-

ian if she were a minor, to marry a particular man. The promise was made to him, or to his father or guardian. At their *sponsalia,* the groom-to-be presented the maiden with a ring and she gave him a present, perhaps a toga of fine cloth. This was the formal aspect of the betrothal, but it was probably of less interest to the participating families than the settlement of the dowry, without which no bride could consider herself respectable. (Nor would many grooms consider her desirable.) If the betrothed couple were very young, the actual wedding might be set some years off. But regardless of the length of the interval between the *sponsalia* and the wedding, the betrothal could be broken off at any time by the bride or her father.

Certain legal requirements had to be met before the wedding ceremony could take place. Both parties or their parents had to give their consent; the bride had to be at least twelve years old, the groom fourteen; neither could be married; and they could not be closely related. There was one other important, though not legal, requirement: The bride had to be acceptable to the household

Clasped hands on 6th-century Byzantine marriage ring were recurrent symbol used until popularity of plain gold circlets prevailed.

gods and ancestors of the groom's family. The Roman family, like the Greek family, was an almost sacred entity and the entrance of an unrelated stranger into its midst was a solemn matter. The ancestors and the gods had to be consulted. A sign of their approval was usually sought in the steaming guts of a sacrificial sheep, although the custom of earlier Roman generations was to look for a sign in the flight of a flock of birds.

Once these conditions had been satisfied, a lucky date was sought for the actual ceremony. Almost a third of the year, including May and the first half of June, was considered unlucky for weddings due to religious ceremonies and holidays occurring during that time. What determined a lucky date was a matter of personal and public superstition.

The evening before the wedding the young bride put away her child's toga and *bulla* (a medallion worn by all Roman children on a chain or string around the neck), dedicating them to the gods of her household in a prayer similar to that offered by Greek brides. The next morning she put on the straight hanging tunic she would wear at her wedding. The bride's mother helped her with her wedding dress, knotting a belt of wool around the tunic with a "knot of Hercules" that could be untied only by the groom. The mother also helped dress her daughter's hair in the traditional style of Roman brides: six locks, possibly braided and always ribboned. To separate the locks, the hair was gently parted with the point of a spear or a comb so shaped. This custom probably recalled the occasional marriages by capture of prehistoric Roman times. Above her locks the bride placed a wreath of flowers and sacred plants that she had picked herself; over all she wore a flame-colored veil to ward off the evil eye.

The dressing of the bride was completed before dawn. The groom, respectfully accompanied by his relatives and friends, arrived just after the *auspices* (ritual sacrifice and omen reading) had been made. He, also, wore a floral wreath and his best toga.

The house of the bride's father, which was almost always the scene of a Roman wedding, was by now filled with guests milling about the open center court *(atrium)* where the ceremony was to take place. The house itself, like an Elizabethan house fifteen hundred years later, was decked with fragrant flowers, leafy boughs, and bright tapestries. After the favorable *auspices* were announced (were they ever found unfavorable at this stage?) the bride and groom appeared in the atrium and the ceremony began. There was a rather self-conscious dignity about the typical ceremony; everything was stately and superstitious. And the Romans, being the Romans, probably took it all quite seriously.

Oddly enough, there was no specific, legal Roman marriage ceremony. All that was required was that the wedding be demonstrated by some kind of public act, like the joining of hands, in the presence of ten witnesses. But a marriage could also be effected simply by the signing of a marriage contract or by the public escorting of the bride to her husband's home. Once such a public ritual had been enacted, it was not legally necessary for the couple to live together as man and wife for their marriage to be valid. Often they did not, especially if very young.

Thus, surrounded by witnesses in the form of friends, associates, and relatives, the young couple performed the wedding ceremony in the public area of the atrium. A functionary called the *pronuba* would begin the ceremony by joining the right hands of the bride and groom. The *pronuba,* by custom, was a woman who had married only once and was still living in good circumstances with her husband. Then the bride spoke the words said by all Roman brides, regardless of the groom's actual name: *Quando tu Gaius, ego Gaia.* The words meant, "When (and where) you are

Gaius, then (and there) I am Gaia," which is to say, "I am the
bone of your bone, flesh of your flesh." (The name Gaius was probably used for its historical associations, but the true purpose of
its use is uncertain.) After that oath, the bride and groom sat
down on adjoining stools at the left of an altar. These stools were
covered with the pelt of the sheep that had been sacrificed earlier.
An offering was now made to Jupiter, this in the form of a wheat
cake, part of which was eaten by the bride and groom. Prayers
also were made to Juno, the goddess of marriage, and other
deities. A kind of altar boy called the *camillus* participated in
these offerings. By custom he had to have living parents, and he

was obviously a precursor of today's ringbearer in symbolizing the hoped-for male child.

When the ceremony was completed, the wedding guests congratulated the couple, and all sat down to a wedding feast in the house. At the end of the meal, the guests were served pieces of the ceremonial wedding cake, much as cake is served today. (Apparently these feasts, like many today, were extravagant affairs. The Emperor Augustus even attempted to limit their cost by law, but, as might be expected, he was unsuccessful.)

The relentless Romans followed the feast with a second, exhaustive set of ritual marriage ceremonies. This consisted of a

Pronuba, mistress of Roman wedding ceremonies, joins right hands of bride and groom in classic frieze. Hymen, winged god of marriage, bears nuptial torch.

mock abduction, a bridal procession, a ceremonial entrance into the groom's house, an initiation ritual there, and, finally, another wedding feast.

In the early evening the bridal procession that was to lead the bride to her new home began to form in front of her father's house. Inside, the first feast was ending with a solemn marriage hymn sung to the new couple. When the song was finished, the groom took the bride from her mother's arms in a mock show of force. To the Romans this act recalled the rape of the Sabine women, a celebrated episode in their history. Modern historians are inclined to explain it as a remnant of the same prehistoric practice of marriage by capture that was recalled by the parting of the bride's hair with a spear point. In any case, everyone at the feast probably enjoyed the mock struggle and all embarked happily on the wedding procession, fortified by wine and food.

By the time the procession began it was dark outside. Thus the torchbearers who escorted the party fulfilled a double function; their torches both lit the way through the black maze of the capital's streets and also symbolized the enduring flame of marriage. With the torchbearers at the head of the procession were the musicians, probably flutists and perhaps a drummer. The light and noise of the procession naturally attracted the attention of the populace. Anyone could join and many probably did, either for the fun of it or in hopes of receiving a small offering of food or money. The bride herself was escorted by two boys, each holding one of her hands, and was led by a third bearing a torch of white thorn which was believed to have power to ward off evil. Behind the bride two women bore a distaff and a spindle as symbols of her future domestic life. The groom was not in the procession; he had slipped away to return to his home so that he could greet his wife when she arrived there.

The bride probably wished that he were with her to protect her from the noisy, ribald crowd. Around her tipsy members of the wedding party sang loud and bawdy marriage songs, a custom adopted from the Greeks. The rowdy Roman populace yelled the traditional wedding cheer, *"Talassio!"* Nobody knew exactly what the word meant but it had a fine sound. Along the way the bride was expected to drop a coin at a street corner as an offering to the gods of the crossroads. (She was also to offer a coin to the groom as a symbol of her dowry and another to his household gods for their favor.)

Finally, reaching her new home, the bride was greeted by the groom, and another of the symbolic ceremonies that the Romans loved so much took place. While the groom scattered nuts to the crowd, the patient bride wound bands of wool, symbols of her woman's work, around the doorposts and anointed the door itself with oil and fat, symbols of prosperity. The wedding party passed by the glistening door, which was then unceremoniously slammed shut to the jostling crowd. The public procession was over. The groom carried his bride across the threshold.

Now that the wedding party was inside, more ceremonies took place. Everyone assembled in the groom's atrium, where he solemnly offered his bride fire and water as tokens of their new life and her new role as wife. The bride then kindled wood in the family hearth; to start the fire she used the white thorn torch that had preceded her on the march. The torch was then thrown to the guests as a lucky souvenir. A prayer was said by the bride and the whole party sat down to another wedding feast, this one at the expense of the groom. After a discreet interval, the new couple retired to the bridal chamber, there sleepily to untie the knot of Hercules.

In the later days of the Roman Empire, it became a literary

fashion to chastise the Romans for their immoral behavior. Virtuous marriages still existed, of course, but divorce was common and the excesses of Nero and his kind seemed to set the style of the age. Tacitus, writing early in the second century after Christ, was a high-born moralist who looked back longingly to the comparatively virtuous days of the Republic. He found Roman society rife with evil and injustice and marriage being mocked. Tacitus tells, for instance, of the bigamous marriage of Messalina, the notoriously wayward wife of the Emperor Claudius, to Silius, one of her lovers:

"I am well aware that it will seem a fable that any persons in the world could have been so obtuse in a city which knows everything and hides nothing, much more, that these persons should have been a consul-elect and the emperor's wife; that, on an appointed day, before witnesses duly summoned, they should have come together as if for the purpose of legitimate marriage; that she should have sacrificed to the gods, have taken her place among a company of guests, have lavished her kisses and caresses, and passed the night in the freedom which marriage permits. But this is no story to excite wonder; I do but relate what I have heard and what our fathers recorded." (*Annals,* Book XI)

Just as Rousseau in the late eighteenth century was to find a contrast to corrupt civilization in the "noble savage," Tacitus saw in the barbarous Germanic tribes the virtues that Rome lacked. Of them he wrote:

"Their marriage code, however, is strict, and indeed no part of their manners is more praiseworthy. Almost alone among barbarians they are content with one wife, except a very few of them, and these not from sensuality, but because their noble birth procures for them many offers of alliance. The wife does not bring a dower to the husband, but the husband to the wife. The

parents and relatives are present, and pass judgment on the marriage gifts, gifts not meant to suit a woman's taste, nor such as a bride would deck herself with, but oxen, a caparisoned steed, a shield, a lance, and a sword. With these presents the wife is espoused, and she herself in her turn brings her husband a gift of arms. This they count their strongest bond of union, these their sacred mysteries, these their gods of marriage. Lest the woman should think herself to stand apart from aspirations after noble deeds and from perils of war, she is reminded by the ceremony which inaugurates marriage that she is her husband's partner in toil and danger, destined to suffer and to dare with him alike both in peace and in war. The yoked oxen, the harnessed steed, the gift of arms, proclaimed this fact. She must live and die with the feeling that she is receiving what she must hand down to her children neither tarnished nor depreciated, what future daughters-in-law may receive, and may be so passed on to her grandchildren." *(Germany and Its Tribes)*

These same warlike people were eventually to help destroy and conquer Rome. Their marriage customs were not to prevail, however, among the conquered people. It was the wedding customs of the Biblical Jews, joined to the laws of Rome, that would be the basis of wedding ceremonies in the western world.

Pompeian wall painting of "Aldobrandine Wedding" may show preparations for a marriage, or portray a Dionysian rite.

Biblical Era: The Marriage Ethic

Our knowledge of wedding customs among the early Jews is limited. The Old Testament is not at all explicit about the need for a wedding ceremony and the account of the creation of Eve in Genesis mentions none. John Milton—like many of his fellow Puritans—was bothered by this omission. In *Paradise Lost* he sought to set the matter right with his own account of Eve's appearance in Paradise:

> "*. . . On she came,*
> *Led by her Heavenly Maker, though unseen,*
> *And guided by his voice, nor uninformed*
> *Of nuptial sanctity and marriage rites.*"

It seems, though, that the actual "wedding ceremony" of the early Hebrews was quite simply the sexual union of the man and woman. Wives were purchased and marriage legally began with the betrothal or agreement to marriage. Betrothals were effected by the payment of money—at least two shekels—by the groom to the parents of the bride in the presence of witnesses. A man who was poor might work for the bride's parents if he did not have the bride price. Jacob earned Rachel and Leah by his labor. Since there is evidence of marriage by purchase in the Bible—Ruth was purchased by Boaz—it is possible that the "bride price" was a legacy of such a practice. After the Exile the bride price was supplemented by the dowry.

All in all, ancient Jewish marriages were dominated by, and conducted mainly for, the males of the tribe. The Biblical Jehovah is an emphatically male divinity and his male worshipers ruled their wives as he ruled them. The head of a family chose his sons' brides, and almost never consulted his daughters about their feelings when the time came for them to marry.

Though there was little to the ancient Jewish wedding ceremony itself, there were a great many rules about what kind of mate was suitable for the Jewish bride or groom. Among these rules were prohibitions against marrying outside the tribe or marrying close blood relatives. Some laws were not always observed in practice, however; according to some authorities, marriages to non-Israelites were not uncommon.

Despite the fact that the wives of the Biblical Jews had not much legal choice in the matter of their fate, they were apparently cherished and well looked after; the famous "Levirate" custom whereby men often married the widows of their brothers, is an example of this concern. Polygamy was acceptable if a man could afford it.

The early Jewish brides had twelve months between their betrothal and wedding in which to gather their trousseau and prepare for marriage. The bridegroom was free from military service during this period. When the wedding was finally celebrated, great feasting and pomp marked it, though the actual ceremony took place in the bridegroom's tent: an event and place later symbolized by the Chuppah, or bridal canopy. The Hebrew word for wedding was "Nissuin," meaning "bringing the wife to the husband's home."

The marriage observances of early Christians took inspiration from the Bible, as well as from the traditions of Rome. The Judeo-Christian wedding traditions that began in Rome have lasted down the centuries, in them we find the origins of our present day weddings.

Middle Ages: Pageantry and Rejoicing

hen in the year 1195 Count Baldwin VI of Hainaut was married to the Countess Marie of Champagne, the people of both provinces rejoiced accordingly. It was an excellent marriage. True, the couple was young: Baldwin fourteen, Marie twelve. But it was a match that allied two noble houses to their mutual advantage. The juvenile bride brought Baldwin an impressive dowry of land and money, and he, in turn, presumably assured Champagne of assistance in its wars with its neighbors. The wedding itself was celebrated sumptuously, with a rich pageantry that typified the noble weddings of the Middle Ages. The marriage was representative, too, in that it had been arranged to aggrandize the power, prosperity, and security of two families. Everyone related to or feudally connected with such a bridal couple had reason to rejoice in their marriage. (The new middle class of town-dwelling merchants and craftsmen rejoiced less perhaps; the wedding might exact special taxes or tribute from them. On the other hand, they might have an opportunity to sell expensive goods to the wedding party. But their feelings mattered little in any case, for this tiny group of townsmen was still a relatively unimportant social element.)

In the feudal, predominantly rural areas of medieval Europe each man, from serf to lord, owed a sacred (and legal) allegiance to someone above him. Kings were responsible to God. There was little social mobility; a man's birth usually determined his rank and fortune for life. The family was the basic social unit in Europe for more than a thousand years, from the fall of the Roman Empire to the discovery of the New World. Within this familial society, a wedding was a highly important event.

When the primary purpose of marriage was to preserve the family, cousins were likely partners, although to prevent inbreeding the church forbade marriage between any but the most distant cousins. At the Vatican Council of 1215 it modified the rule slightly to permit fifth cousins to marry.

Great and small lords looked eagerly among their subjects for marriageable widows or orphaned daughters, for it often was their right to marry off such women and take a share of the dowry for doing so. In the midst of all this financial and familial contracting, the church surprisingly seemed to favor romantic love. It looked upon marriage as a sacrament that husband and wife bestowed upon each other. It sought, although unsuccessfully, to prevent child marriage, demanding that a bride be at least fifteen. It even required that she give her free consent to the match. These injunctions usually were ignored or sidestepped by early betrothals and parental persuasion. In the early Middle Ages, the church recognized the private exchange of vows ("spousals") as an actual marriage, especially when rings, kisses, or even money were exchanged, if such a union was later blessed by a priest. It was not unusual for the church to defend spousal against the wrath of parents and guardians. Such a betrothal is recounted by a priest in the last scene of Shakespeare's *Twelfth Night:*

> *"A contract of eternal bond of love,*
> *Confirm'd by mutual joinder of your hands,*
> *Attested by the holy close of lips,*
> *Strengthen'd by the interchangement of your rings;*
> *And all the ceremony of this compact*
> *Sealed in my function, by my testimony."*

To avoid such impetuous love matches and their dubious financial and social rewards, parents betrothed their children at a very early age. Even infant boys and girls were betrothed and were occasionally raised together. (As late as the nineteenth century, in rural Brittany, betrothed children slept in the same cot.)

Once a likely wedding match had been agreed upon, the betrothal negotiations were begun. Every detail was carefully put in writing, the bride's dowry listed to the last groat. The groom's family, in turn, promised certain rights and protections to the bride, mostly regarding her inheritance. Betrothal negotiations, especially royal ones, often were conducted at some distance. In such cases, where the suitor had never seen the lady in question, he had to depend on secondhand reports. Painted portraits often were requested. But a wise lord would rely on the impartial accounts of trusted friends and servants. Henry VII, the wily widower king of England, was such a lord. When, in 1505, he thought to marry again, a likely prospect seemed to be the plump little widowed Queen of Naples. Henry promptly sent off three trusted ambassadors to the threadbare Neapolitan court. With them the ambassadors carried an order with detailed instructions from the king, commanding them to inspect the queen and her fortune. Among the twenty-four items to be answered were:

Shrewd monarch and cautious lover, Henry VII of England sent marriage ambassadors to Naples to inspect prospective bride. They subjected her to scrutiny which she unfortunately failed to pass.

Anno 1505 20 octaus ymago henrick vir taueris regie illustrissioi
oidinato ɔ hezwani zmik ɔo regie

"Item, specially to mark and note well the age and stature of the said young queen, and the features of her body.

"Item, specially to mark the favor of her visage, whether she be painted or not, and whether it be fat or lean, sharp or round, and whether her countenance be cheerful and amiable, frowning or melancholy, steadfast or light, or blushing in communication.

"Item, to see her hands bare, and to note the fashion of them whether the palm of her hand be thick or thin, and whether her hands be fat or lean, long or short.

"Item, to mark whether there appear any hair about her lips or not.

"Item, that they endeavor them to speak with the said young queen fasting, and that she may tell unto them some matter at length, and to approach as near her mouth as they honestly may, to the intent that they may feel the condition of her breath . . .

"Item, to inquire of the manner of her diet and whether she be a great feeder or drinker, and whether she useth often to eat or drink, and whether she drinketh wine or water or both."

The king also ordered the ambassadors to "diligently inquire for some cunning painter" to portray the queen.

Finally, Henry wanted to know—in detail—just how the young widow was supporting herself.

When the English delegation arrived in Naples it was disconcerted to find that the object of its inspection wore "a great mantle of cloth on her in such wise after the manner of the country that a man shall not lightly perceive anything except only the visage, wherefore we could not be in certain of any such features of her body." Nevertheless, they proceeded undaunted to fill out their master's questionnaire. The queen was not as cooperative as she might have been—the ambassadors had some difficulty in cornering her in order to sample her breath.

Flemish miniature of about 1500 depicts incident from "Roman de la Rose," long allegorical poem expressing erotic element of courtly love.

Et nu wie me stadus
Restant enfranunde

(They finally did and pronounced it clear.) She knew, of course, what they were up to, and wanting the marriage, she naturally sought to remain as mysteriously desirable as possible.

The ambassadors, however, persevered in their assignment and eventually returned to England with a report of a short, "somewhat fat," dark woman of twenty-seven. They also noted that she was large breasted, clear skinned, and amiable. Her lip was free of hair, but, unfortunately, so was her treasury free of money. King Henry turned his amorous eyes elsewhere.

Henry's ambassadors apparently returned without a portrait of the queen, but such paintings were commonly made, even by great artists. Jan van Eyck was dispatched to far-off Portugal on such an errand by Philip the Good, Duke of Burgundy, in 1428. He accompanied royal ambassadors sent to inspect a princess. Some rulers sought to save time by simultaneously comparing several portraits of distant bridal prospects. King Charles VI of France had the same artist paint likenesses of three noble ladies. After some consideration, Charles chose Isabella of Bavaria as the most beautiful of the three. She was not a pauper, either. Charles was still hedging his bet when the betrothed Isabella arrived to marry him. He disguised himself and mingled unnoticed with the Parisian masses that greeted the princess on her entry into the city. The king was knocked about by unknowing constables and eventually returned to his palace, there—finally— to greet Isabella in person.

Greeting a royal bride was always a gala event for a city. The whole town turned out, each group—magistrates, merchants, craftsmen—wearing its special livery. Pageants and plays were staged, dispensations and pardons made, and gifts presented—all amid universal feasting and drinking. The arrival of Princess Margaret of England at Bruges in June, 1468 was such an occasion. She came to marry Charles, Duke of Burgundy, one of the richest rulers of Christendom.

The night before her entry into Bruges, Margaret arrived at the town of Sluis in Flanders. The entire town seemed ablaze. Every house and building was aglow with wax torches. The citizens stood at their doors bearing more torches, and huge bonfires lit the town's squares. Before retiring, Margaret had to watch an interminable mime-pageant staged in her honor. The next morning she was on the road to Bruges.

At the city's gate she was met by the burghers bearing torches like those at Sluis. They presented her with four fine horses in trappings of white damask bordered with blue. The townsmen themselves were colorfully dressed—torchbearers in blue, merchants in crimson velvet, servants in crimson cloth, and others in black damask. The princess was led through tapestry-hung gates into the city. There the streets were lined with thousands of loyal Burgundians, cheering and throwing flowers in the princess's path. After some progress the procession came to a stop again. There was another elaborate pageant for the princess to witness, this time on the theme of marriage in myth and history. It began with the wedding of Adam and Eve as performed by God.

Eventually, the weary princess arrived at the royal apartments. She was greeted there by the Duke's old mother, and then the Duke himself appeared. By the account of a witness, Charles seemed enchanted with the princess. He kissed her several times before all the attending nobles, returned to his palace, came back to kiss her again, returned to the palace and came back to kiss her yet again. The match appeared to be a happy one.

It was likely, though, that whatever love and romance Margaret found after her marriage would not come from Charles. The romantic love of which the medieval troubadours sang was the

Miniature painted a century
after the fact celebrates marriage
of John I of Portugal to
Philippa of Lancaster
in typically ornate royal wedding
of Middle Ages. Left: Detail
of couple joining hands.

domain of married women and their courtiers. It was sensual or spiritual, but not marital. "Courtship" was just that—a courtier's pursuit of his lady's love; adultery was implied, but rarely took place. A great deal of talking and debating was done, however. "Courts of love" were formed for the diversion of fashionable nobility. The "trials" and debates were often written and conducted by troubadours and poets or philosophers. At the time when courtly love was at its height, whole cities participated in celebrating it. In his book *Mediaeval Culture,* Karl Vossler tells us: "In June of the year 1283, at the festival of St. John in Florence . . . a social union was formed, composed of a thousand people who, all clad in white, called themselves the Servants of Love. They arranged a succession of sports, merry makings and dances with ladies; nobles and bourgeois marched to the sound of trumpets and music in wild delight to and fro, and held festive banquets at midday and at night. This Court of Love lasted nearly two months, and it was the finest and most famous that had ever been held in Florence, or in all Tuscany."

Beneath all of the romantic and spiritual symbolism expressed in courtly love was a basic eroticism that consistently asserted itself. The *Roman de la Rose,* which the historian Johan Huizinga called a "glorification of seduction," dominated medieval popular literature for two centuries. Seemingly contrasting with the *Roman* was the knightly tradition of "pure" spiritual love. It was this opposition that furnished the theme for the many courts-of-love debates. (It is worth noting that the central dramas of the two great legends of the Middle Ages—Tristan and Iseult and the Arthurian saga—involve adultery.) However, this ambivalence was carefully kept out of marriage arrangements. Huizinga declares: "In the very matter-of-fact considerations on which a match between noble families was based there was little room

Love's darts are shivered on chastity's shield (left) in allegorical painting of Florentine school. Above: Love was stiffly portrayed in medieval art, but amour was fostered in courtly circles.

for the chivalrous fictions of prowess and of service."

The betrothal ceremony of the Middle Ages was almost as solemn and important as the wedding itself. Performed before the church door or porch, it consisted of an exchange by the bride- and groom-to-be of *de futuri* vows to marry each other. These vows were blessed by a priest and were sometimes pronounced over holy relics. Betrothal rings might be exchanged by the couple as the priest declared them engaged. This ceremony was witnessed by parents (or guardians) and relatives, and after it ended the whole group, led by the priest, entered the church to attend mass. The church porch would also be the scene of the wedding ceremony, since the interior of the church itself was for worship only. Of the Wife of Bath in *The Canterbury Tales*, Chaucer wrote:

> *"She was a worthy woman all her live,*
> *Husbands at the Church door had she five."*

The church door was also thought to be the right spot for the assignment of the dowry, which was done before the marriage ceremony. An English wedding contract tells us:

"Robert Fitz Roger (in 1278) entered into an engagement with Robert de Tybetol, to marry, within a limited time, John his son and heir, to Hauisia the daughter of the said Robert de Tybetol, to endow her at the church door on her wedding-day with lands amounting to the value of one hundred pounds per annum."

The betrothal rings worn by the newly engaged couple usually were engraved with short poems, or "posies," not unlike the one scornfully described in *The Merchant of Venice*:

> *"——a hoop of gold, a paltry ring . . .*
> *whose posy was*
> *for all the world, like Cutler's poetry*
> *Upon a knife, 'Love me, and leave me not.'"*

Wedding customs of Middle Ages can be traced in numerous paintings of "Marriage Feast of Cana," such as this 15th-century Spanish work.

Sometimes these rings, like the later Elizabethan rings, would consist of two or three circlets bound together ("gimmel rings") with two- or three-line posies engraved on them. The names of the betrothed couple might also be engraved on the rings.

Betrothal entitled the young couple to some coveted privileges. They could eat out of the same porringer as they sat together at meals. The man might write love poems to his intended bride or, if he were rich, he might hire a jongleur to compose them. The two were now permitted to take walks together and, if they were members of the nobility, she might give him one of her colored silk sleeves or stockings to hang on his lance at jousts. She might also cut off a lock of her hair for him to tie around his helmet. In such ways the betrothed passed the forty-day period during which the required "banns of marriage" (public notices) were posted—a time when any irregularities (such as a previous betrothal by one of the parties) could be discovered. It was also the time for whatever romance the bride-to-be might experience. She would soon be married and absorbed in the duties of medieval wifehood.

It has been said that the main reason marriage was so highly esteemed in the Middle Ages was because the church and society made it almost impossible for married couples to obtain a divorce. The same was true for betrothals. An engagement was not easily broken. Having been performed in front of a church or in the chantry and blessed by a priest, it was almost a sacrament. It could be annulled only by the church and the costs involved were very high.

Midsummer was the favored time for medieval weddings. The summer harvest had been gathered and the days were warm. Good weather was important, because the wedding itself and the celebration that followed usually were held out-of-doors.

The eve of a wedding found all concerned preparing their costumes and the food to be served. These required special thought and care, for the medieval wedding was as much a public pageant as a private celebration, and would be severely judged by all of the spectators, each of whom considered himself a connoisseur of marriage ritual.

There was no traditional wedding costume for the bride or groom. Often a bride would wear the same costume she had worn to the Easter festival. A noble bride would probably have a special dress made for the wedding, but such an extravagance was beyond the means of most girls. The right dress, old or new, had to have certain attributes. Color was important, red being a favorite. White was not yet the nearly universal choice it is today. Vivid color was the ideal. A noble French bride of the thirteenth century might wear a violet pelisse trimmed with ermine over a chemise of saffron-tinted linen. Over the pelisse a coat of green silk with long sleeves and a train that flowed behind, and over all a mantle of royal purple silk. Shoes of vermilion leather and a saffron veil would complete the costume.

Noble brides wore their finest jewelry, peasant brides their favorite flowers. A brooch and crown were common wedding jewelry; even the peasant bride in the Brueghel *Wedding Feast* painting wears a narrow circlet on her head. A royal bride would have worn her coronet.

In the Middle Ages the groom was almost as splendidly dressed as the bride, certainly as colorfully. How such a bride and groom wore their costumes was also important; noble vestments required noble bearing.

When all were dressed and ready, the wedding procession to the church could begin. This procession, the ceremony, and the celebration were the three principal parts of a wedding and each

*Amid symbols of marriage, Giovanni Arnolfini
and Jeanne Cenami perform own wedding in Bruges in
1434, a moment preserved by Jan van Eyck.
Detail of mirror shows two witnesses facing couple.*

was carefully planned and executed. The procession was led by jongleurs or musicians, playing flutes, harps, cymbals, horns, and drums. (Among peasants, the procession to the remarriage of a widower might be led by a "burlesque serenade" of pots and pans.) After the musicians came the bride, her hair hanging loose or braided down her back as a sign of her virginity. She would walk or, if noble, be borne by a sumpter mule or a richly caparisoned horse. The bride's father usually escorted her. The mother, other relatives, godparents, and friends—the latter in order of rank—followed. The groom and his family and friends were also part of the procession. At the church portal the procession was met by the priest, who performed the wedding service there, in view of the public.

Before the vows were exchanged, an official recited the amount and contents of the bride's dowry in a loud voice, so that no one would be in doubt as to the precise terms of the marriage contract. The couple then exchanged their marriage vows. An English manuscript missal of Richard II's years of reign (1377-1399) has these vows:

The groom: "I take thee to be my wedded wife, to have and to hold, for fairer for fouler, for better for worse, for richer for poorer, in sickness and in health, from this time forward, till death us do part, if holy church it will ordain, and thereto I plight thee my troth."

As he placed the wedding ring on the bride's finger, the groom said: "With this ring I thee wed and this gold and silver I thee give and with my body I thee worship, and with my worldly chattels I thee honor."

The bride's vow was similar to the groom's except that she also vowed to be "bonny and buxom in bed and at board." This, unfortunately, was later changed to "meek and obedient."

The ring which the groom gave the bride usually was engraved like the betrothal rings. Saint Louis IX of France, for instance, gave his wife Marguerite a ring with the three chief loves of his life engraved upon it (in order of precedence): "God, France, Marguerite." The usual inscriptions tended to be less portentous than Louis's, however. No medieval wedding could be valid without the placing of a ring on the bride's finger and the circlet itself had a mystic importance that made it a powerful symbol. (When Charles the Bold, Duke of Burgundy, annexed the dukedom of Normandy he was symbolically "married" to the province by the bishop of Lisieux and given a "wedding" ring to mark the event. Later when Louis XI usurped Charles' dukedom, he had the ring broken on an anvil at Rouen, in Normandy, in the presence of assembled nobles.)

When the spectators at a medieval wedding saw the bride receive the ring they gave each other hearty slaps and pushes, the better to remember the event. There were no parish or government records of marriages and the blows were part of "the ritual of witness" so important for the recognition of a wedding's validity. In the sixteenth century the church at the Council of Trent prescribed that a priest and two witnesses be present at a marriage. (The benediction of a priest was not essential from the church's point of view—the consenting bride and groom bestowed the "sacramental grace" of marriage on each other. It was secular society, not the church, which first insisted on the formality of a church wedding.)

The wedding ceremony concluded with the ritual tossing of money over the heads of the newlyweds into the amiably jostling crowd of spectators. Medieval account ledgers are full of items like £2 (about $350) thrown by order of the king at the marriage of Isabella, daughter of Sir Hugh Despenser, to Richard, son of

Edmund, Earl of Arundel, in 1317. Forgotten in the scramble for the coins, the wedding party made its way sedately into the church to hear the wedding mass.

The bride and groom first sat in the choir while the priest pronounced a special blessing on them. They were covered by a marriage pall symbolic of their future life together. Any children the couple might have had out of wedlock before the marriage could be placed under the pall with them and thereby legitimized, a custom that nicely expressed the acceptance of illegitimate children by medieval society.

During the wedding mass the couple might share a cup of blessed wine and a blessed wafer. Then they walked to the altar where the groom received the "kiss of peace" from the priest and in turn kissed the bride. Sometimes, the bride might also spin a little wool or flax with a distaff to symbolize her devotion to her approaching domesticity. Finally the mass was over and, after some two hours of ritual, the party was free to celebrate. The procession home was much like the one to church, but probably noisier, happier, and less dignified. There might be a brief stop

Hymeneal figure dominates festivities at wedding of Duke of Savoy to Catherine of Austria. Canopied marriage bed is behind array of gifts at left. Jousts, parades, and banqueting enliven scene.

while the bride and groom entered the church cemetery and prayed at the graves of their ancestors to seek the blessing of the dead.

When the bride and groom entered her father's house they were showered with seed, corn, or grain by their friends to cries of "plenty! plenty!" The seed, of course, symbolized fertility for the bride and fortune for the couple. In an age of frequent death and dire poverty, this ritual was often performed in vain. "In some parts," wrote a thirteenth-century observer, "I have seen how, when women came home from church after a wedding, others threw corn in their faces as they entered their house, crying plenty! plenty, yet for all this, before the year was past, they remained poor for the most part, and had no abundance of goods whatsoever."

Shoddy substitutes for seed were sometimes used in the cities. Bologna passed a statute in 1259 forbidding the throwing of "snow, grain, paper-cuttings, sawdust, street-sweepings and other impurities" at weddings.

The wedding feast now began. The house of the host would have been cleaned and decorated, the richer homes with silk hangings and treasured tapestries. Both rich and poor bridal homes were strewn with roses, lilies, and other fragrant flowers.

> *"There neat in splendor, pompous in array,*
> *Each spacious hall and princely chamber lay.*
> *Rich furniture in costly order placed;*
> *Never was seat of marriage nobler graced.*
> *Spread every table; every office stored;*
> *With delicates to load the bridal board."*

That scene from the Student's Tale in Chaucer's *Canterbury Tales* is evidence of the medieval emphasis on wedding feasts—"delicates to load the bridal board" were very important for the success of any nuptial celebration. But eating was not enough, there must be music, drinking, and dancing, too.

> *"And now the palace gates are opened wide;*
> *The guests appear in order, side by side,*
> *And placed in state the bridegroom and the bride.*
> *The breathing flute's soft notes are heard around,*
> *And the shrill trumpets mix their silver sound;*
> *The vaulted roofs with echoing music ring,*
> *These touch the vocal stops, and those the trembling*
> *   string . . .*
> *Meantime the vig'rous dancers beat the ground,*
> *And songs were sung, and flowing bowls went round;*
> *With od'rous spices they perfumed the place,*
> *And mirth and pleasure showed in every face."*

This noisy scene is described by Chaucer in the Merchant's Tale. Exactly what the revelers ate and sang and drank and danced varied from place to place, but it was sure to be rich and bawdy and intoxicating and hectic.

Gifts were both given and received by the guests at a medieval wedding feast—mostly received. Mantles, goblets, gloves, rings, cloth, jewelry—these were the kinds of presents expected by the invited guests. Moreover, each gift had to be presented with a small speech.

At a noble wedding celebration in summertime, the bride and groom, their families, and the highest-ranking guests were usually seated at a table within an open-fronted tent. The other guests were served at trestle tables in the open air, as was the whole wedding party at humbler celebrations. The local peasants, if not invited, would ring the outskirts of the area until, made bold by beer, they invaded the festivities. A thoughtful host made provisions for these people in planning the wedding feast, for a new marriage was traditionally a time for generosity.

The father of the bride had been for some time purchasing and storing the great quantities of food and drink he would be expected to serve his many guests. Variety was as important as quantity at a wedding feast. Whole roast stag was the favorite dish, with other varieties of game also favored. Domestic cattle ("butcher's meat") was not as popular as it is today. Pork, not beef, was the most common meat. Fish was a familiar daily food and not especially prized at a wedding feast, but it was served, nevertheless, along with an incredible variety of fowl. A typical "pastie" (pie) might contain three partridges, six quail, a dozen thrushes, bacon, sour grapes, and salt, all covered with a flour crust. Vegetables and breads were served with the various meats, fish, and fowl, and everything was accompanied by strong spices, especially pepper. Honey and fruit served as sweets, for sugar was still an expensive rarity. Thus, all around, the bridal feast

Lo Spagnuolo's "Marriage at Cana" has mundane air of contemporary 17th-century wedding feast in artist's native Bologna.

was a panorama of bubbling kettles, steaming vats, and turning spits—the whole tended by an army of cooks and servants.

To go with the food there were tuns of wine and barrels of barley beer. Drinking loosened the formality of the party and quickly induced that "merriness" so important to a medieval wedding. The more beer and wine drunk, the more frenetic the dancing, the bawdier the songs and jokes. Bawdiness was a part of most European wedding celebrations, high and low, down to the eighteenth century. It was in the performances and ballads of the hired jongleurs and troubadours, and in the songs sung to the bride and groom as they retired. Not that bawdiness set the tone of the celebration; it was merely an accepted flavoring. The new couple sat sedately at the table of honor and were served with dignity and respect. Everyone listened carefully to the long, romantic ballads that the troubadours sang. As they listened from their flower-wreathed chairs, the bride and groom ate from the same porringer and drank from the same goblet.

When everyone was full of food and wine, the dancing began. To the accompaniment of the musicians who had led the wedding procession, the bride and groom and their guests whirled in circles

while holding hands or more quietly performed an ancestral version of the minuet in which the men and women advanced, bowed, and retired to the rhythm of the music.

The happy round of eating, drinking, singing, and dancing was often further enlivened by such lighthearted medieval pranks as the presentation of a large pastie filled with perhaps a hundred live thrushes which, when released, were immediately killed by a dozen hunting hawks. Or a female dwarf might be plumped on the nuptial table as a humorous gift for the bride. With such innocent fun the celebration continued long into the night.

At last it came time for the newlyweds to be escorted to the bridal chamber, led by the priest who would remind them of their duty to God and accompanied by the guests who sang ribald epithalamia to remind them of their duty to their future family. Dressed for bed, the bride and groom would kneel while the priest blessed the "nuptial couch," which, in the Middle Ages, was al-

most sacred ground. The bed would often be strewn with roses
and censed like an altar. Sometimes the newly married pair would
abstain from intercourse the first night (or even the first three
nights) in honor of the Virgin Mary, to whom they prayed until
they fell asleep.

The morning after the wedding, the couple would attend mass
again and say prayers for the success of the marriage. The wedding celebration would continue for two or three days (sometimes
two or three weeks) and the bride and groom would probably
return to it, for at that time there were no honeymoons.

They had only their wedding rings as records of their marriage. There were no wedding certificates as we know them,
though the presence of witnesses was prescribed by church law.
In fact, it was that requirement which brought about the creation
of the most beautiful and valuable marriage "certificate" in history: the Arnolfini wedding portrait by Jan van Eyck.

Giovanni Arnolfini was a prosperous Italian merchant of the early fifteenth century. He lived in the rich northern European city of Bruges. When he wished to marry, Arnolfini sought a girl of his own nationality. He found her in Jeanne Cenami, born of Italian parents in Paris. Jeanne joined Arnolfini in Bruges, where they had decided to be married.

Giovanni and Jeanne had few or no friends and relatives in Bruges, so a church wedding seemed unreasonable. Since the church did not then require that a priest perform the marriage and held that a man and woman could marry themselves, the

Arnolfinis chose to perform their own wedding by exchanging vows in privacy.

In that respect the Arnolfini wedding was not especially unusual. There were many such private weddings during the Middle Ages. What made the Arnolfini wedding memorable was their unique decision to memorialize their union with a painted wedding portrait. Moreover, they chose as the painter one of the greatest artists of all time, Jan van Eyck.

In northern Europe during the fifteenth century a group of Flemish painters had evolved an incredibly realistic style of painting. Jan van Eyck was the first and greatest of these painters.

Rubens on Marriage: Golden apple of discord sent by uninvited goddess roils divine guests at wedding of Peleus and Thetis, worried pair at right. Left: Sketch for series of allegorical paintings of Henri IV's marriage to Marie de Medici.

Most of the subjects he and his contemporaries portrayed were religious scenes from the Bible. A secular subject like the Arnolfini portrait was extremely rare. A closer look, however, reveals religious overtones even in this painting. When, in 1434, van Eyck received his commission and began to paint the wedding portrait, he consciously and carefully sought to include in the picture symbols of religious significance.

The poses of Giovanni and Jeanne, the objects that surround them, the setting itself all symbolize the importance, strength, and deep meaning which medieval men and women attached to the institution of marriage. The couple stand in the center of their bridal chamber, a room which had religious importance in the Middle Ages; the bed itself, as we have seen, was often blessed and sanctified by a priest on the wedding night. Yet the time of the painted scene is day, not night, for the wedding was performed in the sight of God, whose all-seeing presence is symbolized by the single blazing candle in the chandelier above the Arnolfinis. (The candle also echoed the traditional "marriage candle," the Christian substitute for the ancient wedding torch of the Greeks and Romans.) Beneath the chandelier, Giovanni Arnolfini, his left hand clasping his bride's right, raises his right forearm in a gesture of affirmation, implying that he and his bride have just recited their vows. Church law at that time required only those actions together with the placing of a ring upon the bride's finger to constitute a legitimate marriage. The church also recommended witnesses, if possible, and in fact there are two in the painting; reflected in the mirror are two figures facing the wedding couple, witnesses of the nuptial scene. One of the figures is almost certainly Jan van Eyck himself. Moreover, van Eyck signed the painting in an obvious and elaborate manner just above the mirror. It was very unusual for a painter to sign his work in the Middle Ages. Painters then were craftsmen, not "artists" as they are today. Then it was no more natural to sign a newly-made painting than to sign a newly-made barrel, and when a picture was signed it was usually in the form of the artist's name followed by the Latin word *fecit,* meaning so-and-so "made this." But van Eyck has signed the Arnolfini painting *"Johannes van Eyck fuit hic"*—"Jan van Eyck was here," meaning he was there as a witness. This great painting is unique in its purpose and signature; that it is unique is a pity, for the idea was a fine one.

Van Eyck and his patrons were truly medieval in their fondness for symbols. The painting is almost a compendium of those ambiguously meaningful objects. The dog at the couple's feet, for instance, was a well-known symbol of marital faithfulness; similar canines nestle against the feet of many sculptured ladies reclining beside their husbands on lids of medieval tombs. The discarded shoes are thought to refer to the Biblical injunction to "Put off thy shoes from off thy feet, for the place whereon thou standest is holy ground" (i.e., the sanctified bridal chamber). Paradise lost and the fruit of forbidden knowledge are recalled by the oranges on the windowsill, while the cherries on the tree outside the window denote the season of midsummer. The crystal beads hanging next to the mirror and the shiny surface of the mirror itself refer to the virgin purity of Mary, mother of Christ, while ten small scenes around the mirror display His passion. Purity must be combined with practicality, so domestic industry and virtue are proclaimed by the broom hung on the bedpost. And, lastly, but perhaps most importantly, the little statue of Saint Margaret on the arm of the chair above the bride's hand modestly but unmistakably invokes the patron saint of childbirth. The couple's thoughtful piety has left us a superb evocation of what the wedding meant to medieval Christians.

Norimbergensis virgo Patricia nuptiis ornata.

Costume showed female status in 16th century. Clockwise from top left: Danzig wife, Nuremberg fiancée, Venetian wife, Frankfurt fiancée, Leipzig virgin, Cologne wife. Opposite: Nuremberg virgin.

arly in the twelfth century a love-sick Spaniard wrote a poem expressing his longing for an uncooperative lady. The verse was in the fashionable troubadour vein: "Live on, though thy lips drop honey for others to sip; live on, breathing myrrh for others to inhale. Though thou art false to me, till the cold earth claims her own again, I shall remain true to thee. My heart loves to hear thy nightingale's song, though the songster is above me and afar." The composer of these impassioned words was not a popular troubadour, nor was he a courtier. He was a serious Spanish-Jewish scholar of some renown, named Moses Ibn Ezra. The fact that his poetry resembled that of the troubadours in more than coincidence.

One of the remarkable things about the Jews of the Middle Ages was the extent to which they drew on the ideas and customs of the predominant Christian culture while preserving the essentials of their own heritage. Sometimes the Jews borrowed ideas that seem strangely incongruous to their own strongly religious culture. The Spanish Jews, for instance, were known to enliven their more ambitious bridal processions with mock jousting tourneys, complete with armored knights, prancing horses, and splintering lances. What the martial Spanish Christians may have thought on seeing such an unlikely display is not known, but they probably enjoyed it immensely; medieval crowds loved pomp and pageantry of any kind.

The similarities between the essential marriage customs of the medieval Christians and Jews shows the continuance of the Judeo-Christian tradition that started in the early days of Christianity. Both Christians and Jews believed that consenting men and women could wed themselves by recitation of vows and the exchange of a ring. The requirement of a rabbinical blessing for a wedding was a late medieval development, as was the Christian requirement of a priestly blessing.

The basic form and sequence of the usual Jewish wedding at the height of the Middle Ages resembled the basic Christian form and sequence: A match was agreed upon, a marriage contract was drawn up, a betrothal ceremony was witnessed (often, in the cases of both Jews and Christians, just before the wedding); there was an elaborate bridal procession, a religious wedding ceremony, and a prolonged and energetic celebration. Skilled musicians performed at the wedding banquets and, if the banquet continued into the Sabbath, as it often did, Christian musicians were brought in to continue the playing. The skill of Jewish musicians was well-known and their playing was often sought, in turn, for Christian banquets.

The European Jews of the period also had distinctive marriage customs of their own which reflected the nature of Jewish life and character. There was, for instance, the widespread practice of consulting a *shadchan,* a professional matchmaker, in

order to arrange a satisfactory marriage. Because communities were widely scattered and travel was very difficult in the Middle Ages, it was hard for marriageable Jewish men and women to meet. It was customary in some areas for families to bring marriageable children with them to the great trade fairs. But this kind of meeting was too brief to be really satisfactory. The *shadchan* remained the best source of bridal prospects.

Marriage was looked upon as essential for all healthy Jews, and the reasons for this were religious as well as social. Israel Abrahams, in his book *Jewish Life in the Middle Ages,* explained the reason for this: "Jewish tradition had it that the Messianic era could not dawn until all the souls created by God from the primeval chaos had been fitted to the earthly bodies destined for their reception here below. To hurry on the great day, mothers and fathers eagerly joined their children in wedlock, each mother dreaming perhaps that in the child of her own offspring God would deign to plant the soul of the longed-for redeemer."

In an age of religious persecution, the uncertainty of their lives and fortunes prompted the Jews to arrange child betrothals and even child marriages when the right match suggested itself and while the bride's dowry remained intact. Here, again, a good *shadchan* met the needs of the community by finding a suitable bridegroom with comparative dispatch and thoughtful discernment. The *shadchan* was sometimes a rabbi, but more often— because mobility was essential to a *shadchan's* function—he was a traveling merchant. Like the Roman *pronuba* he charged a fee for his services. The fee was usually fixed at between one and two per cent of the bride's dowry and was generally paid on the drawing up of the marriage contract, though sometimes a *shadchan* was forced to wait until the wedding was accomplished before he was paid. The matchmakers worked hard for their fees, shuttling back and forth between interested parties, arranging meetings, settling disagreements, extolling virtues, and advocating practicality. The rewards were not inconsiderable, however. Besides his fees, the *shadchan* might also gain high respect in the community he served.

Although the status of the Jewish woman had improved greatly since Biblical days, she was still largely a passive pawn in the

German Jewish groom of 18th century
gives ring to bride under supervision of rabbi (right).
Portuguese groom of same period (below)
smashes glass from which he and bride have drunk
sacramental wine. Both brides wear veil mourning
Jewish diaspora. Zither and viols make music.

serious business of matrimony. Even though the Talmud stated that "A man must not betrothe his daughter while she is a minor: he must wait till she attains her majority, and says, 'I love this man,' " in practice, a girl's husband was usually chosen for her according to the liking of her parents or guardian. By the thirteenth century, many Jewish girls were being betrothed in their thirteenth year, the earliest age permissible by Talmudic law. The grooms were usually older, about seventeen, but they, too, were sometimes as young as the bride.

Once a suitable mate had been fixed on by a family with an unmarried daughter, the *shidduchin,* or friendly negotiations, began. If the parties reached an agreement, a banquet of celebration was given by the groom-to-be. He could afford to be lavish, since this would probably be his only big expense in connection with the wedding. The bride's father, as is customary today, paid for almost everything else. A marriage contract was drawn up; it usually contained a clause that provided for a fixed penalty payment if either party chose to cancel the betrothal.

Except among the medieval Jews of Greece and Turkey, the engagement ring was worn by the man, not the woman. In Germany, the bride's father presented the groom with a ring; the bride received her ring on the morning of her wedding day. Traditionally, it could contain no gems, for they might deceive the bride as to its real value. It usually had a tiny replica of the destroyed Temple of Jerusalem or of a synagogue on the crest of the hoop and a hollow space within the hoop to contain a sprig of myrtle. This ring was probably a symbol of the ancient bride-price of Biblical times.

Wedding presents of high value were given to the couple upon their betrothal. Many of the illuminated medieval prayer books and copies of the Haggadah in museums today originally were wedding presents. The bride usually received an expensive girdle from the groom, hair ornaments and jewelry from others.

Once the young couple were betrothed, the families sought an auspicious date for the wedding. There could be no marriages between Passover and Pentecost; this custom may have stemmed from the Roman superstition that forbade marriage in May. It was also thought that a wedding should coincide with a full moon. Many Christians also shared this superstition and it is possible that the belief may have been related to the ritual marriages of prehistory and their concurrence with important phases of the moon. Superstition was enough to determine most couples in their choice of a nuptial date. As in ancient times, Friday was the most popular day for a wedding; the seven-day celebration that followed would end fittingly on the eve of the Sabbath.

On the appointed day, the wedding was inaugurated by a procession to the synagogue. This could be, as it was in Spain, a lively affair, but it was also usually dignified—at least in Europe. Stern Western rabbis were horrified by the antics of the medieval Egyptian Jews, whose bridal processions were considered to be shamefully dissolute.

In Biblical times the Jewish bridal procession led directly to the bridal tent where the marriage was promptly, and almost publicly, consummated. In the Middle Ages, when the religious ceremony was interposed between the procession and the consummation, the memory of the nuptial tent lingered on in the form of the *chuppa*. This was the canopy under which the bride and groom made their vows. Another ancient custom, this one adopted from the Romans, was the greeting of the bridal pair with torches early in the morning of their wedding day. The classical custom of tossing nuts and grain in the bride's path also was adopted by the Jews, who cried, "Be fruitful and multiply," as they did so.

Courtship in Renaissance Italy
was often a formal matter. Above and in
enlarged detail at right, suitor and
maiden converse demurely at a casement.
Any such attentions were considered
a sign of marital intentions.

It was in the wedding ceremony following the procession that the Jews expressed the somber side of their past and present. In the so-called "reminder" customs of the wedding they commemorated the destruction of Zion, the dispersal of the Israelites, and the subsequent history of racial grief. The bride herself covered her wedding finery with a white shroud of mourning. (This color could also be taken to signify her presumably spotless virtue, but this evidently was not its primary meaning.) In Germany, the Jewish groom also wore a hood of mourning over his Sabbath clothes. The hood was drawn back during the ceremony and the rabbi rubbed ashes on the groom's head: another reminder rite.

Both the bride and groom often wore bridal crowns or wreaths on their heads. These crowns could be elaborately constructed of roses, myrtle, olive branches, semiprecious stones, and threads of gold and crimson, but they could not contain real gold or silver. Such trimmings were forbidden in remembrance of the persecution of the Jews by the Roman Emperor Vespasian.

The bride and groom fasted during the morning before the ceremony, which usually took place in the synagogue after the regular morning service. The groom was already in the synagogue when the bride, decked with garlands and jewelry, appeared at the door to the sound of music. She was escorted by the rabbi and the elders of the congregation, who placed her beside the groom on a raised platform in the center of the temple. The rabbi sang a blessing and asked the witnesses if the bride's ring had some value. They invariably replied that it did. The groom then said to the bride, "Behold thou art consecrated to me by this ring, according to the law of Moses and of Israel." The rabbi intoned a benediction after witnesses had vouched for the validity of the marriage contract. The bride and groom concluded the ceremony by smashing the glasses from which they had drunk the sacramental wine. Originally the glasses were thrown against the synagogue wall, but later they were stamped underfoot. Then, as one medieval observer put it, "the assembled company rushed at the bridegroom, uttering expressions of joy, and conveyed him before the bride to the wedding house." There was no doubt then about which of the bridal pair was the more honored. However, the bride, as always, had her special moments.

After the "reminders" and general solemnity of the ceremony the wedding party wanted joy and laughter to dominate the ensuing celebration. Originally, it had been the custom of the rabbi to deliver a sober discourse on the virtues and responsibility of marriage to the banquet guests, but this ·was so little to the liking of tipsy celebrants that eventually the rabbinical sermon was exiled to the synagogue and delivered within the dignified context of the wedding ceremony. The *marshallik,* or jester, supplied the desired mood of hilarity at the wedding feast. He was a distinctive character in medieval weddings, especially in Eastern Europe. Sometimes ribald, sometimes insulting, the *marshallik* cracked jokes, sang songs, and delivered impromptu poems and satiric speeches.

It was widely believed by medieval Jews—and Christians, for that matter—that if the groom placed his right foot over the bride's left foot during the wedding ceremony, he would have effective dominance over her during their marriage. Naturally brides sought an effective antidote. Many of them undoubtedly found it in the advice of one writer, who counseled the bride who had been superstitiously trod upon to wait patiently through the day for the wedding night. Then, as the consummation was about to take place, she was to ask the preoccupied groom for a glass of water. *She* was guaranteed dominance after that.

Part II. Love and Courtship

genteel, slightly ludicrous connotation attaches to the word "courtship" today. It summons up visions of blushing virgins, awkward swains, anxious mothers, frowning fathers, swooning, flattery, passionate letters, furtive glances, spooning, petting, wooing, and other assorted Victorian bric-a-brac. Today, wives (and husbands) are still sought and won (or lost), but the game has become less formal and less ritualized than it was half a century ago. It has become less painful and perhaps it has also become less exciting. Above all, it has become, like marriage itself, much more a private affair between a man and a woman, and much less a public happening before watchful families and friends. Anguished love has become the property of teen-agers and the profit of pop musicians. Fathers have lost control over the marital fate of their children; what was once a matter of careful parental calculation and businesslike negotiation has become one of ineffectual observation and slightly apprehensive optimism. In fact, the seeking and winning of a wife or husband has become such an informal, haphazard affair that the word "courting," with its implications of special behavior, etiquette, and social boundaries, seems inappropriate. Words like "dating," "going steady," or, simply, "going with" now describe a male-female relationship that may or may not be heading toward engagement and marriage. What separates these terms and others like them from the term "courting" is their flavor of privacy, vagueness of intention, and social mobility—three qualities that were rarely associated with courtship prior to this century.

Despite the decline in formality and conformity, courting is still with us. In essence, it is the attempt to attract, to allure, and to gain affection. Women must be sought, one way or another, and if, as today, they are often themselves the suitors, it is something they do by necessity rather than desire. The change

Preceding pages: Culmination of successful Renaissance courtship is depicted in Lorenzo Lotto painting of groom placing ring on fourth finger of bride's left hand.

in the manner of courting has not come from a change in the nature of woman, but from a change in society. Throughout history the form of the courtship has depended upon the form of the society in which it took place and, especially, the status of women within that society. The less status women had the less likelihood they would be courted.

Primitive societies, with their elaborate codes of behavior, use of symbolism, and prescribed routines for acquiring a bride, bear some resemblance to Victorian society. The primitives also share a trait with most birds and many animals: The males are much more colorfully arrayed than the females—all the better "to allure, to attract, and to gain affection."

In those primitive societies where brides are purchased, women have an economic value beyond their basic functions as sexual companions and son-bearers; they are also wood-gatherers, food-growers and harvesters, cloth-weavers, and cooks. Tribal men usually limit their activities to hunting and fighting. When they seek a wife—as every man must in almost every society—they look for a healthy girl, capable of bearing many children and working very hard. She must, of course, belong to the right tribe or family or clan or phratry or cousin-group. Where women are plentiful the suitor will seek a dowry for taking the girl off her father's hands, and may take several wives. Romance and love do not usually enter the picture.

In a traditional tribal group, marriage negotiations can be a fascinating blend of ritual and hard bargaining. For example, when a Ugandan wants to marry a girl, he does not approach her, but rather goes to her elder brother and paternal uncle to arrange a marriage. During this meeting the girl is called in and asked to pour beer; if she pours, it means she doesn't object to the suitor and the negotiations continue without her.

The Ugandan suitor is expected to offer a good price for the girl in cows, goats, salt, cloth, and jewelry.

Sometimes there is a recognized price scale for brides. Among the Kaffirs six cattle is regarded as about the minimum price for a homely girl with a bad temper, and thirty cattle are enough for an energetic beauty. Among the egalitarian Togolese, at one time, a standard price for all brides prevailed: $16 in cash and $6 in goods.

Today, with the rapid social homogenization of the world, these practices are dwindling or disappearing. Inflation has recently sent the bride prices soaring in New Guinea. As much as $5,600 is being paid for one woman. The government there has temporarily "frozen" the bride price and hopes to set a standard soon. The newly independent African governments are often unsympathetic to the hallowed marital customs of their citizens. In the Ivory Coast, where men with incomes of $150 a year were paying as high as $50 for their wives, the bride price and even polygamy have been abolished. With the adoption of a money-based economy in modern tribal societies, the possession of an extra wife or two has become more of a status symbol and less an economic necessity.

Marriage by capture was once an acknowledged, if not accepted, practice in many parts of the world. Some nineteenth-century historians, viewing wife-capture as basically savage, believed that it was the first form of marriage. This theory has since been rejected as invalid, but the fact remains that such disparate groups as the ancient Hebrews, Australian aborigines, Russian Slavs, and North American Indians occasionally captured women for wives. One thing these groups had in common was a view of wives as economic property. The father owned his daughter until he sold her to a suitor. We still speak of a father

Neoclassical title page of British periodical devoted to matrimonial concerns shows Cupid and Psyche being transported to Temple of Marriage.

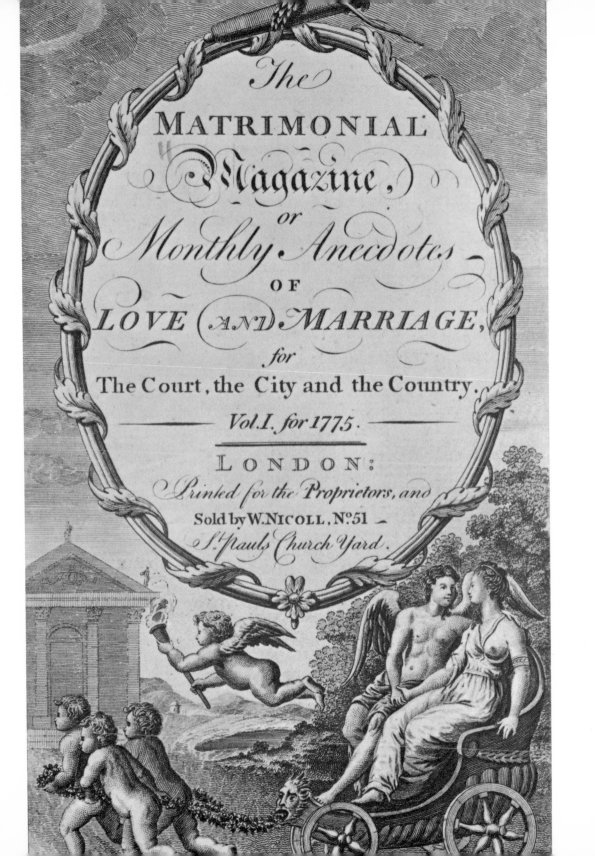

The
MATRIMONIAL
Magazine,
or
Monthly Anecdotes
OF
LOVE AND MARRIAGE,
for
The Court, the City and the Country.

Vol. I. for 1775.

LONDON:
Printed for the Proprietors, and
Sold by W. NICOLL, Nº 51
St Pauls Church Yard.

Bowing suitor calls on well-chaperoned Dutch woman in 17th-century work by Gerard Ter Borch. Visit is not a surprise.

Hogarth's "Marriage Contract" betroths a reluctant lass with large dowry to vacuous young gentleman with family tree but no money.

as "giving his daughter away" in marriage (though, as a modern father of the bride is painfully aware, that is not exactly the case today). However, in some societies, much of the bride pric received by the father was spent on the wedding.

In Europe and later in America, the purchase of brides eventually became obsolete. By the eighteenth century many women were beginning to have something to say about their future husbands. In the East this has begun to happen only recently. Not only have eastern brides traditionally been permitted no choice in their marriages, but often they never saw their husbands until the wedding ceremony.

The status of woman has always been lowest in eastern civilizations. Herodotus, writing more than two thousand years ago, tells us that once a year the Babylonians assembled the marriageable girls of a town in one place. Men seeking wives gathered in a circle around the women, and an auctioneer began offering the girls for sale. "He began with the most beautiful," Herodotus writes. "When she was sold for no small sum of money, he offered for sale the one who came next to her in beauty." The homely girls in the group were finally offered to the men who would accept them for the sake of a small marriage portion; a dowry was then, and still is, a kind of bribe.

During the ensuing two millenniums the status of most Asian women rose scarcely higher than the Babylonian level. In China the Confucian view of women fixed their position for twenty-five hundred years. For Confucius, woman's only duty was to obey. In childhood she obeyed her father, in marriage she obeyed her husband (and mother-in-law), and in widowhood she obeyed her son. Courtship was beside the point. "How sad it is to be a woman!" wrote the ancient poet, Fu Hsuan. "Nothing on earth is held so cheap." Certain early Christian church fathers looked upon women as born sinners, tools of the Devil. Much the same attitude could be found among the Buddhists. Hindu men were cautioned by the Laws of Manu to avoid women if possible and never to sit in a secluded place with even their nearest female relative. The Japanese marriage manual, called *Kaibara* and a part of the traditional trousseau of every self-respecting bride, counseled wives to cultivate the virtues of obedience, chastity, mercy, and quietness. The Moslems had no higher view of women and kept their wives and daughters secluded. Throughout the East, then, the generally accepted view of women as passive, child-bearing, house-running chattels did nothing to foster pre-marital romance or courting. What a suitor sought was a family's consent, not a daughter's love, for the family was the most important social unit.

Intricate kissing game
(opposite) entrances elegant young
people of early 19th-century
England, while sportive Dickensian types
above, by Cruikshank, mix
music with amour.

The actual suitor in the Orient usually was the groom-to-be's father. As in most business transactions, middlemen flourished; they found suitable brides and grooms and negotiated contracts. The criteria applied by such professional suitors were hardly the same as those of modern suitors. The Laws of Manu offer extremely detailed descriptions of the good and bad qualities to be sought and avoided in prospective brides and grooms. For instance, a girl with red hair, bandy legs, and moist hands was to be avoided like the plague, according to Manu, but, to be fair, it is not likely that she would be much sought after anywhere. In the public baths of the Turkish Empire, unmarried girls wandered about nude before prospective mothers-in-law. The latter, if impressed, gave detailed reports to their sons and husbands. Again, this was not exactly courtship as we know it.

Many Indian, Japanese, Chinese, and even Arab daughters were undoubtedly given some chance to preview their suitors before the wedding, and sometimes a wedding was even called off if the bride or groom remained adamantly opposed, but this only reinforced the general view that as little contact as possible should be had between future brides and grooms.

When, by chance, a man and woman actually had the opportunity to fall in love and wanted to marry each other, there was usually a feeling that the match was unwise. *Gandhara* (love) marriages were denounced in India. In Korea, until 1910, a love marriage was illegitimate and subject to severe punishment.

It should be pointed out that traditional eastern marriages were remarkably stable and that divorce, where possible, was rare. Love and esteem often grew out of arranged marriages, and who is to say that the husbands and wives of these matches were not happier than modern western couples? But the East today is changing and rapidly adopting western-style love marriages. The Japanese lead this trend, having been the first to break the old pattern by permitting "seeing sessions" in which a boy and a girl are allowed to inspect each other furtively in the presence of relatives. In modern Japan the collision of romantic love and parental objections has resulted in an epidemic of lovers' suicides, preferably by a dual leap into the crater of Mount Fuji. For such extreme examples of frustrated courtship in the West, we have to look back to the Middle Ages and the tension between spirituality and duty on the one hand and romantic love on the other.

Parental authority and the prohibitions of the church and society against extramarital sex were prevailing forces in ancient and medieval Europe. Most marriages were, we know, arranged. Though love affairs must have occurred now and then, it was probably rare for them to culminate in marriage, especially among members of the upper classes. Weddings were negotiated and legalized by binding contracts, and it was the duty of the young to comply with the wishes of their elders. Such marriage contracts made the intentions of the parents legally binding on their children. These arranged marriages continued to be common until the nineteenth century in western Europe.

England was apparently the first country to show signs of breaking the old pattern. As early as 1724 an English gentleman could write patronizingly of Sweden, where "the Parents, without consulting their Children, match them as they think fit, and wealth is chiefly consider'd in the Affair: The poor Girls have not so much as an opportunity of being courted and admir'd, or the Lover the Pleasure of communicating his flame...."

But even in England most marriages continued to be arranged, though the boy and girl were often consulted and usually had met each other. English royal marriages were consistently arranged

well into modern times, sometimes with very unhappy results.

Regardless of its financial, social, and legal advantages, the practice of arranged marriages did not create a climate in which courtship was likely to flourish. In Europe from the time of the Greeks to the eighteenth century, courtship usually meant a period of mutual examination by a couple after their arranged betrothal. Once a wedding was agreed upon there were certain formal duties to be performed by the groom: He must call upon the bride; he must present her with gifts (and she present gifts to him also); he must write to say complimentary things to her; he and she must find, through the difficult medium of innocuous, formal conversation—usually in the presence of chaperons or parents, friends, relatives, duennas, guards, servants, nuns, or priests—what their mutual opinions and intelligences might be. They could also discretely inspect each other. Sometimes a betrothal could be broken off by one or both of the parties if there was a serious objection. Sometimes objection did no good.

Sensing, perhaps, the hollowness of their own courtship etiquette, the upper classes became interested in the apparent sincerity of country courtship. Paintings of peasants clumsily courting blushing maids became prized by eighteenth-century aristocrats. The nobles of Bourbon France loved to trip about parks in the costumes of shepherds and milkmaids. It was, perhaps, a touching attempt to regain lost innocence. Yet there is a smugness in the expressions of these painted figures—as we see them in the pictures of Watteau, Lancret, and Boucher—that belies their guises. In most instances this style of courtship did not have marriage as its goal. In fact, the institution of marriage was apparently in a state of alarming decline by this time.

In the sixteenth century, under the reign of the Tudors, men extolled the institution of marriage. Such books as *A Discourse*,

Circumspect Victorian courtship involved genteel conversation and flowery flattery. Couple here pretends interest in album.

Of Marriage and Wiving by Alex Niccholes set forth the joys of marriage in glowing terms: "...in thy *Marriage*, the very name thereof should portend unto thee *Merry-age*, thou not only uniteth unto thy self a friend, and comfort for society, but also a companion for pleasure, and in some sort a servant for profite too, for a wife is all these...." The Elizabethans loved courtship and, as we have seen, reveled in its many Tudor forms. Something, however, happened in the next hundred years. With the Puritan revolution, much of the joy seemed to go out of love, and marriage, too, for that matter. The Puritans put a cloud over love and the rakes of the Restoration put a cloud over marriage.

With the decline of the old values, marriage became less of a social necessity. Many bachelors began openly to rejoice in their singleness. Wooing and winning were proper goals for such men, but marriage seemed like a sentence to prison. The Restoration poet Thomas Flatman forcefully expressed this view in his poem "The Bachelor's Song":

> *"How happy a thing were a wedding,*
> > *And a bedding,*
> *If a man might purchase a wife*
> > *For a twelve-month and a day!*
> *But to live with her all a man's life*
> > *Forever and for aye*
> *Till she grow as grey as a cat,*
> *Good faith, Mr. Parson, I thank you for that."*

Preachers and women deplored such an attitude. Men, in their huge, curled wigs and lacy clothing, were becoming far too absorbed in themselves. Women, still intent upon marriage, fought back. An antibachelor pamphlet which appeared in London in 1703 explained its purpose in its lengthy title: *The Levellers: a Dialogue between two young Ladies, concerning Matrimony; proposing an*

Act for Enforcing Marriage, for the Equality of Matches, and Taxing single Persons; with the Danger of Celibacy to a Nation.

The battle raged on in urban conversations and contemporary literature. However, as far as the vast number of ordinary, unfashionable people were concerned, love, courtship, and marriage had changed very little by the end of the seventeenth century.

Love, for instance, was still mistrusted. The arranged match remained the dominant form and the same old marriage goals of increased fortune and higher social standing persisted. For the gentry, marriage negotiations usually began when the children were still very young. Most girls from such families were married before they were eighteen, and marriages at fifteen were not uncommon. Boys were only slightly older when they married. There was, of course, little or no chance for courtship. Nor was it missed.

Engaged Dutch couple standing by mirror receives felicitations of relatives and friends. Servitor with tray will later pour spiced nuptial wine.

The brief Elizabethan sunshine was gone. Marriage was a very serious affair and premarital love was suspect. The best basis for a happy marriage was friendship—and that ideally would develop after, not before, a wedding.

A great amount of advice on choosing a wife was written during the sixteenth, seventeenth, and eighteenth centuries, and most of it was very sober stuff about the good qualities of a virtuous bride. Aside from the usual moral virtues cited in these works, simple good health was highly valued. Until comparatively modern times, a large number of young wives never survived their first pregnancy, and each additional pregnancy was a new danger. Young women were unhealthily restricted in their interests and activities, and tuberculosis was a common cause of death among them. Widowers were at least as common as widows. So life was too full of perils and uncertainty for such an important act as marriage to be governed by the fancy of love. And after all, weren't most women pretty much the same?

Samuel Johnson, musing on a woman he might have married, was asked by Boswell if he did not suppose "that there are fifty women in the world, with any of whom a man may be as happy as with any one woman in particular?" To which Johnson replied, "Ay, Sir, fifty thousand." Boswell, sensing that his mentor had more to say on the subject, then asked if Johnson "was not of the opinion with some who imagined that certain men and certain women are made for each other; and that they cannot be happy if they miss their counterparts." "To be sure not, Sir," Johnson replied. "I believe marriages would in general be as happy, and often more so, if they were all made by the Lord Chancellor, upon a due consideration of the characters and circumstances, without the parties having any choice in the matter."

Johnson's sentiments—and they were probably popular sentiments—were certainly practiced during the settlement of the New World across the Atlantic. In Pilgrim America, the state of courtship was very low.

Marriage in the Massachusetts Bay Colony was imperative for all men and women. It was a practical economic necessity and an aid to survival in the rugged wilderness. It was often a legal as well as a social requirement. Bachelors and unmarried women were ridiculed, the men being put to humiliating tasks such as killing blackbirds and crows.

In such an intensely practical atmosphere, love was naturally scorned. Parents arranged the marriages of their offspring in as businesslike a way as their counterparts were doing in Europe and Asia. A Massachusetts woman had no right to choose her own husband without the consent of her parents or guardian.

When a marriage was arranged, the banns had to be proclaimed before the whole village congregation. Weddings were commonly held eight days after a betrothal, but even in Puritan New England the devil found willing followers; contemporary preachers railed against the apparently popular acceptance of betrothals as a license to sexual lust.

The gaudy clothing in fashion in Europe at the time was also strictly prohibited in Massachusetts. Law courts specifically banned the wearing of "silver, gold, and silk laces, girdles, hat bands, etc." Courtship, when it actually could occur in such an atmosphere, tended to be abrupt and unromantic, the legend of John Alden and Priscilla Mullens notwithstanding.

If courtship in early New England tended to be plain and straightforward, it was systematically bypassed in French Canada. Unlike the English colonies, New France was settled by men and women who came there separately, not as married couples. The French king did his best to supply the men with wives,

Bizarre faculty of "An Elegant Establishment for Young Ladies" teaches posture, painting, music, and dance, among other arts designed to win a husband. Sign behind eloping couple seen through window says: "Man traps are set in these premises."

Early 19th-century swain courts damsel with quatrain which asseverates that he prizes her "guiltless hand" more highly than gold.

and shiploads of girls from poorhouses and farms arrived regularly in the middle of the seventeenth century.

Peasant girls were preferred for their hardiness, but even wellborn ladies sometimes came to marry officers. Nuns accompanied the girls as chaperons on the voyage and then settled down as missionaries in the wilderness.

The contemporary historian LaHoutan wrote a vivid description of the arrival of a bridal vessel: "Several Ships were sent hither from France with a Cargoe of Women of an ordinary Reputation, under the Direction of some old stale Nuns, who rang'd them in three Classes. The Vestal Virgins were heap'd up, (if I may so speak) one above another, in three different Apartments where the Bridegrooms singled out their Brides, just as a Butcher does a Ewe amongst a flock of Sheep. In these three Seraglio's, there was such Variety and Change of Diet, as could satisfy the most whimsical Appetites; for here was some big, some little some fair, some brown, some fat, some meagre. In fine, there was such Accomodation, that everyone might be fitted to his Mind; And indeed the Market had such a Run, that in fifteen Days' time, they were all dispos'd of. I am told, that the fattest went off best, upon the Apprehension that these being less active, would keep truer to their Ingagements, and hold out better against the Cold of the Winter."

The governor of New France gave discharged soldiers a bounty for taking a wife, and he presented gifts to new couples. Bachelors often were penalized as they were in New England. If a man did not choose a wife within fifteen days after the arrival of the first group of imported girls, he was likely to incur prohibitions against hunting, fishing, trading with the Indians, or going into the woods at all. Fathers were responsible for the marriages of their sons and daughters; if any were unmarried at the age of sixteen their fathers were liable to be fined. In such a busy climate, tender courtship was a casualty.

By the eighteenth century, colonial America was better able to provide a setting for love and courtship. Boys and girls still usually married the mates their parents chose for them, but the atmosphere was not as grimly businesslike as it had been earlier. Some Americans did, in fact, engage in a particular form of courtship that was unique in its comfort, scandalousness, innocence, and sensuality: bundling.

The delight of rural New Englanders, bundling was denounced and ridiculed by city-dwellers, preachers, and all those of "high moral tone." There was even disagreement as to what it was. It fascinated some observers (especially Europeans) and repelled others (especially Americans). Those who indulged swore that it was harmless, informative, necessary, and, moreover, pleasurable. (Pleasure was not necessarily considered a virtue in colonial America, so this aspect was not stressed.) Bundling, it was explained, was simply a way for young men and women to court in private and get to know each other before a marriage was decided upon. In hard-working New England there was still little leisure and even less privacy for courtship. The winter evenings were cold and fuel expensive. What more logical, then, than that a young man join a young woman in her bed? Both would wear their underclothes or nightshirts, of course. Sometimes there might even be a board to separate them. The custom had long been practiced by peasant farmers of England, Wales, Scotland, and Holland, as well as America. It may have been introduced to America by the Dutch settlers of New York, but it was in New England that it flourished.

Some cynics claimed that the whole of New England, particularly Cape Cod and Nantucket, was aswarm with the by-products of bundling. There seems no doubt that very often one thing led to another under the patchwork quilts of a bundling bed. It also seems clear that much bundling was done with an innocence of which only Puritans could be capable. The practice was righteously and loudly defended by virginal girls and their mothers when any clergyman was rash enough to attack the practice. Around 1800, one such minister composed a somber piece entitled "A Poem Against Bundling. Dedicated to Ye Youth of Both Sexes." Through a dozen or so verses the Puritan poet attacked the vice and hypocrisy he saw in bundling. Each excuse for the practice was ticked off with merciless scorn. The poet concluded with a stanza aimed at those who would not or could not heed his advice:

> *"Down deep in hell there let them dwell*
> *And bundle on that Bed.*
> *There burn and roll without control,*
> *'Till all their lusts are fed."*

But the minister was beating a beast that was already half dead. Bundling had been rendered a mortal blow as early as the 1780's when several famous poems ridiculed it. These ballads appeared as popularly circulated broadsides and in the widely read *Farmer's Almanac*. A dozen lines from one of them sums up the antibundling position.

> *"Young miss if this your practice be,*
> *I'll teach you now yourself to see:*
> *You plead you're honest, modest too,*
> *But such a plea will never do;*
> *For how can modisty consist,*
> *With shameful practice such as this?*
> *I'll give your answer to the life:*
> *"You don't undress, like man and wife,"*
> *That is your plea, I'll freely own,*
> *But whose your bondsmen when alone,*
> *That further rules you will not break,*
> *And marriage liberties partake?"*

Bundling was never more that a local practice. Courtship in the eighteenth century consisted mainly of polite and chaperoned visits, calls, and occasional outings. Parents of the new middle classes allowed more freedom to their young marriageable children, but they still sought suitable mates for them and courtship remained hardly more than a postbetrothal get-acquainted period.

However, the old marriage customs were changing and by the 1800's most English and American girls were free to choose

their husbands. The Romantic Era helped bring about that emancipation by idealizing women in terms that Samuel Johnson would have scorned.

Even in Elizabethan times—though England was awash with flowery sentiments of love—women were still regarded as second-class citizens. "The wives speciall duty may fitly be referred to two heads: first, she must acknowledge her inferioritie: secondly, she must carry her selfe as an inferior," wrote William Whately in his *A Bride-Bush* in 1619. Such sentiments were not particularly conservative in those days and it is unlikely that any reader—even among the women—took exception to it. But by the beginning of the nineteenth century things had changed tremendously. The Romantic view of women was in fashion and by midcentury it had reached its Victorian apogee. Purity was all, sex almost unmentionable. Love was edifying. "What a re-

Francis Jukes' aquatints of 1787 illustrate difference between ardent "Courtship" (left) and enervating "Matrimony."

"First Class—the Meeting": Miss Melting Eyes crochets quietly, knowing that after one more story from the seafaring stranger, Papa will invite him home for dinner.

finer is love! how it purifies us from ourselves, strengthening age and ennobling the mind, pointing out a God-like motive, and a nobler idea to all we do, to all we think, to all we say, making us strong, courageous, and true! Oh, the greatness of the capacity to love! Surely it is the noblest gift we have!—sacred because it is God's gift,—sacred, because it is the life in heaven."

Those inspiring words were written by Henry Southgate in *The Way to Woo and Win a Wife* in 1876. Southgate was an indefatigable compiler of sayings about love and marriage. He emphasized the positive side of love to his Victorian readers, but also warned of the lurking danger: "Let the essence of thy love be pure; for if one unhallowed breath be breathed upon its flame, it is gone forever, and leaves only a sullied vase, its gentle light crushed out in shame forever."

The Victorians did not need to be told what "unhallowed breath" meant. The proper nineteenth-century lover might idealize a woman *ad nauseam,* but he must never touch her with base thoughts in mind. Southgate, in the great tradition of courtship counselors, offered some gemlike expressions for his readers' use. He called them "Sunny Sentences, To Her I Love Best." They were apparently to be dropped into the lover's conversation in order to brighten up his own embarrassed mutterings. Here are a few:

> *"Your hair is as sunny as your heart."*
> *"Your kind, deep, dewey eyes."*
> *"Thy sweet dumb eloquence of beauty. . .*
> *commands me without authority."*
> *"My armorial bearings are the red and*
> *white rose quartered in your dear face."*
> *"Thou mirror of heaven."*
> *"Thou breathing star."*
> *"My very being warbles into songs of thee."*
> *"The choir of your love keeps me in tune."*

These were not atypical Victorian exuberances. The literature of the period is full of similar expressions. Southgate himself quotes with approval the archetypal Victorian poet and lover, Robert Browning, on a woman's glance:

> *"O! tis so chaste, so touching, so refined,*
> *So soft, so wistful, so sincere, so kind!"*

Now that women were so highly prized, it was only fitting that courtship be elevated (a favorite Victorian word) accordingly. Women expected it. An increasingly larger number of them now had something to say about their suitors, and they were determined to be sought.

Many men were sadly unprepared for their new roles as

winners of hearts, rather than bargainers for wives. They were particularly lacking in knowledge of the gentle arts of persuasion and flattery. They needed help. Fortunately, there were a great many—like Henry Southgate—who were willing to give it.

Like a flood tide in spring, the nineteenth century opened with a wave of how-to-woo-and-win books that increased in quantity and variety in the next hundred years. These volumes had a wide and grateful audience, much as cookbooks do today. There were recipes for any kind of courtship problem. There was, for instance, the pressing matter of courtship by mail.

Every nuance of love and intention could be contained in the words of a well-phrased letter. The witless swain had but to copy out the printed letter, changing (one hopes) the minor details of name and circumstance to his purpose. Best of all, the letters printed in these books were artfully divided into samples representing the various social classes. Those supposedly written by the gentry were arch in phrase, oblique in meaning, and tedious in effect. *The Lover's Instructor or The Whole Art of Courtship Rendered Plain and Easy*, a handy volume that appeared in London in 1810, proudly offered such a letter on its first page of examples:

LETTER 1. AN ASSURANCE OF LOVE.

Madam,

There is now no minute of my life that does not afford me some new argument how much I love you. The little joy I take in every thing wherein you are not concerned; the pleasing perplexity of endless thought which I fall into, wherever you are brought to my remembrance; and lately, the continued disquiet I am in, during your absence, convince me sufficiently, that I do you justice in loving you, so as woman was never loved before.

The sample letters offered to tradesmen were plain and to the point. But best of all were the letters supposedly composed by peasants and laborers. These documents were as heavily comic as they were outspoken. They often suggest a hack writer's mimicry of his social inferiors, rather than an "honest" laborer or peasant writing of his feelings. But many of the latter undoubtedly copied the book letters for their own use, if not always the ones intended for them. Two such letters are also offered in *The Lover's Instructor*:

LETTER XLVI

THOMAS COLE, TO MARY JOHNSON. AN APPOINTMENT OF MARRIAGE.

Dear Mary,

I have long been in love with you, but was afraid to tell you. When I go with you to Dobney's, or Sadlers Wells, I am almost like a fool, and altogether unfit for company. I think of you all day, and at night I dream of my dear Mary. I am well settled in work, and my wages are eighteen shillings every week. You and I can live on that, and I shall bring it home untouched on Saturday evening. I will not go to any alehouse, but as soon as my work is done, return home to my dearly beloved Mary. I hope, my dear, you will not be angry, for I am really in love. I cannot be happy unless you are mine. I was afraid to mention this to you, but if you will leave an answer at my lodgings, I will meet you next Sunday, after dinner, at the Shepherd and Shepherdess, when we will take a walk to Hornsey-House, and drink tea. How happy shall I be to hear from my charmer; but a thousand times more to think she will be mine.

I am, my dear, your real lover,
Thomas Cole.

The Lover's Instructor was kind enough to offer its own answer to its own letter.

LETTER XLVII

MARY JOHNSON, TO THOMAS COLE. OBJECTIONS.

Dear Tom,

I received your very kind letter, but I don't know what to say in answer. Although I would be glad to marry, yet you men are so deceiving, that there is no such thing as trusting you. There is Tom Timber, the carpenter, and Jack Hammer, the smith, who have not been married above six months, and every night come home drunk, and beat their wives. What a miserable life is that, Tom, and how do I know but you, like them, may get drunk every night, and beat me black and blue before morning! I do assure you, Tom, if I thought that would be the case, I would scrub floors and scour saucepans as long as I live. But possibly you may not be so bad, for there is Will Cooper, the brazier, and Jack Trotter, the ass-man, who are both very happy with their wives; they are both home-bringing husbands, and have every day a hot joint of meat and a pot of beer. I know not yet what I shall do, but as I like a walk to Hornsey, I will meet you at the Shepherd and Shepherdess, on Sunday after dinner, and then we will talk more of the matter.

I am, dear Tom, your most affectionate servant,

Mary Johnson.

Victorian ladies tended to be just as independent of their suitors in real life as they were in novels. They were determined to pick and choose, and their requirements for a mate were stern. He must be both a romantic lover and a practical man of affairs—a rather hard bill for most men to fill.

The writer Thomas Carlyle, for instance, was a true son of

the Romantic age, but his beloved Jane Welsh was quick to spot his impracticality early in his courtship of her. This Victorian lady answered Carlyle's passionate letter of proposal ("for you do love me, deny it as you might; and your spirit longs to be mingled with mine and mine with yours") as follows:

"My Dearest Friend,——I little thought that my joke about your farming Craigenputtock was to be made the basis of such a serious and extraordinary project. If you had foreseen the state of perplexity which your Letter has thrown me into, you would have practised *any* self-denial (I am sure) rather than have written it. But there is no use in talking of what is *done-- Cosa fatta ha capo*! [The thing done has an end!] The thing to be considered now is what to *do*.

Ceremonial costumes indicate betrothals of Polish girl (far left) and Dutch maiden of 1811 (above left).

Currier & Ives, those indefatigable commentators on 19th-century American life, show bland, look-alike couples in throes of a lovers' quarrel (opposite) and reconciliation.

"You have sometimes asked me, did I ever think. For once in my life at least, I have thought myself into a vertigo, and without coming to any positive conclusion. However, my mind (such as it is) on the matter you have thus precipitately forced on my consideration, I will explain to you frankly and explicitly as the happiness of us both requires.

"I love you, I have told you so a hundred times; and I should be the most ungrateful and injudicious of mortals if I did not; but I am not *in love* with you; that is to say, my love for you is not a passion which overclouds my judgement, and absorbs all my regard for myself and others. It is a simple, honest, serene affection made up of admiration and sympathy and better perhaps, to found domestic enjoyment on than any other. In short, it is a love which *influences,* does not *make* the destiny of a life.

"Such temperate sentiments lend no false colouring, no 'rosy light' to your project. I see it such as it is, with all the arguments for and against it; I see that my consent under existing circumstances would indeed secure to *me* the only fellowship and support I have found in the world; and perhaps, too, shed some sunshine of joy on *your* existence which has hitherto been sullen and cheerless; but, on the other hand, that it would involve you and myself in numberless cares and difficulties; and expose *me* to petty tribulations, which I want fortitude to despise, and which, not despised, would imbitter the peace of us both.

"I do not wish for fortune more than is sufficient for my wants; my natural wants, and the artificial ones which habit has rendered nearly as importunate as the other; but I will not marry on less, because in that case every inconvenience I was subjected to, would remind me of what I had quitted; and the idea of a sacrifice should have no place in a voluntary union. Neither have I any wish for grandeur. The glittering baits of titles and honours are only for children and fools. But I conceive it a duty which every one owes to society, not to throw up that station in it which Providence has assigned him; and having this conviction I could not marry into a station inferior to my own with the approval of my judgement, *which* alone could enable me to brave the censures of my acquaintance.

"And now let me ask you, have you any *certain* livelihood to maintain me in the manner I have been used to live in? Any *fixed* place in the rank of society I have [been] born and bred in? No! You have projects for attaining both, capabilities for attaining both, and much more! But as yet you have *not* attained them. Use the noble gifts which God has given you! You have prudence (tho' by the way this last proceeding is no great proof of it), devise then how you may gain yourself a modest but *settled* income; think of some more promising plan than farming the most barren spot in the county of Dumfriesshire. What a thing that would be to be sure! You and I keeping house at Craigenputtock! I would just as soon think of building myself a nest on the Bass Rock. Nothing but your ignorance of the place saves you from the imputation of insanity for admitting such a thought. Depend upon it you could not *exist* there a twelvemonth. For my part, I would not spend a month at it with an Angel. Think of something else then, apply your industry to carry it into effect, your talents to gild over the inequality of our births; and then—we will talk of marrying. If all this were realised, I *think* I should have good sense enough to abate something of my romantic ideal, and to content myself with stopping short on this side idolatry,—at all events I will marry no one else. This is all the promise I can or will make. A positive

engagement to marry a certain person at a certain time, at all haps and hazards, I have always considered the most ridiculous thing on earth: it is either altogether useless or altogether miserable; if the parties continue faithfully attached to each other, it is a mere ceremony; if otherwise, it becomes a galling fetter riveting them to wretchedness and only to be broken with disgrace.

"Such is the result of my deliberations on this very serious subject. You may approve of it or not; but you cannot either persuade me or convince me out of it. My decisions when I *do* decide are unalterable as the Laws of the Medes and Persians. Write instantly and tell me that you are content to leave the event to time and destiny, and in the meanwhile to continue my Friend and Guardian which you have so long and so faithfully been,—*and nothing more.*" (The following year, 1826, Carlyle

Before last half of 19th century such scenes as these of couples embracing would have been unthinkable as popular art. Victorians valued mistletoe as good excuse for kissing.

became considerably more than friend and guardian to Jane Welsh; they married and in time settled at Craigenputtock.)

Women like Jane Welsh now insisted on certain standards of courtship and propriety, and the ardent but uninformed lover was wise to consult a comprehensive handbook such as *The Lover's Companion, A Hand Book of Courtship and Marriage,* which appeared in America in 1850.

The *Companion* contained detailed advice for every step of the proper courtship. First of all, a young man should ask a girl's parents for permission to "address her" before ever actually talking or writing to the girl herself. Even if approval was given, it was unwise to make oneself too familiar. "When a young man is an accepted suitor, he should pay the lady such attentions as are graceful and becoming, without being excessive," the *Companion* ruled. "Frequent visits are unwise, render the visitor troubleness and liable to reflections, which the lady even-

tually shares with him. They produce, too, that undesirable familiarity which oftener lessens, than increases esteem." Love letters should be sensible and not too revealing.

There was no question of intimacy. Undue familiarity could only produce "indifference if not disgust." Moreover, a lady's character "like the down of a peach, will endure no blemish."

The feelings of people unfortunate enough to have to witness a courtship had to be considered too: "Lovers would do well to remember that while courtship is the most absorbing of all occupations *to them,* it is the most insipid, and when too manifest, the most distasteful to others."

Finally, the *Companion* warned of the continued existence (under a new and fascinating name) of our old friend, the insincere suitor: "Young men frequently amuse themselves by playing with the feelings of a young woman. They visit them often, they walk with them, they pay them diverse attentions, and after giving them an idea that they are attached to them, they either leave them, or, what is worse, never come to an explanation of their sentiments. This is to act the part of a *dangler*, a character truly infamous."

Fortunately for the Victorian lover of an offbeat frame of mind, there were other, less stiffnecked courting guides. *The Young Ladies' and Gentlemen's Hymeneal Instructor or, the Philosophy of Love, Courtship and Marriage,* another American handbook of the mid-nineteenth century, made the interesting suggestion that if a suitor was to form a true estimate of his love, he would be wise to "call upon her suddenly and at an unexpected time—he will be able thus to form some tolerable estimate of her every-day domestic neatness and habits." This was indeed American ingenuity, but it is hardly likely that the author of *The Lover's Companion* would have approved.

*Love's contretemps:
Girl's father
uptilts chaise to
cool off
lover, while sisters
(below) make public
spectacle of
their affection
for same man.*

Lovers who scorned the fevered romanticism of the period found sensible solace in the pages of an English courtship manual by "A Lady." The authoress, after expressing approval of the decline of seven-year courtships, went on to condemn secret, romantic courtships with their "stolen interviews, stolen kisses, broken vows, deep-drawn sighs, home-brewed sonnets, despairing ejaculations, elopements to Gretna, hysterics and smelling bottles." With cool foresight, she advised against putting anything into a letter that the writer would not want read in court.

In America and England, at least, no bashful and ignorant lover needed to despair of learning how to go about the business of courtship in the nineteenth century. Even the most basic of courtship practices, such as kissing, were painstakingly rehearsed and described in elementary texts such as Henry T. Finck's *Romantic Love and Personal Beauty,* an English volume of 1887.

Finck was a thoroughgoing student of love. No aspect of it, no matter how subtle, escaped his clear-eyed attention. The table of contents of his book offers such chapters as: "Evolution of Romantic Love," "Cosmic Attraction and Chemical Affinities," "Emotional Hyperbole," and—Finck at the top of his form— "Kissing—Past, Present and Future." In this last chapter, Finck undertook to explain the subtleties of kissing as an art:

How to Kiss

"Kissing comes by instinct, and yet it is an art which few understand properly. A lover should not hold his bride by the ears in kissing her, as appears to have been customary at Scotch weddings of the last century. A more graceful way, and quite as effective in preventing the bride from 'getting away,' is to put your right arm around her neck, your fingers under her chin, raise the chin, and then gently but firmly press your lips

Coy English couple of 1860's finds trysting place in bosky dell of photographer's studio.

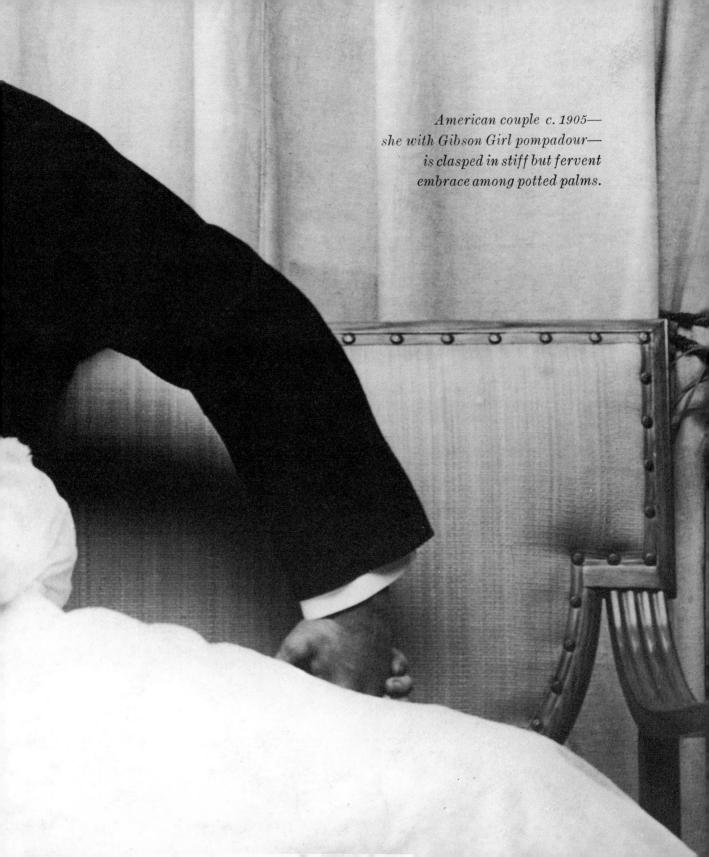

American couple c. 1905—
she with Gibson Girl pompadour—
is clasped in stiff but fervent
embrace among potted palms.

Valentines: Saccharine German postcard, c. 1900 (above), murmurs, "Your enchanting look gives me happiness." Elaborate and lacy creations like that opposite were American favorites.

on hers. After a few repetitions she will find out it doesn't hurt, and become gentle as a lamb."

Again, it is doubtful if the author of the more conventional *Companion* would have approved.

The nineteenth century was, of course, the century of science and progress. All things were capable of improvement, including marriage. The emperor Napoleon himself proclaimed as much: "Marriage in no way owes its origin to Nature...Therefore marriage can be subjected to that gradual process of improvement which everything belonging to mankind seems to undergo."

It was inevitable, then, that science should eventually discover love. The pseudoscience of phrenology was extremely popular

with the Victorians; it allowed them to discreetly caress each other's cranial bumps and thereby discover their true characters. For most people, phrenology was probably just a pleasant pastime, but for others it was a matter of seriousness. "Discard phrenology, and the most effectual guiding staff through the quick-sands of courtship is lost to you," wrote one scholar.

Inevitably, electricity also shocked some people into awareness of its amatory power. Magnetism, especially, fascinated the Victorians. Just as an iron filing could be inexorably pulled to a small magnet, so could a reluctant loved one be pulled to a suitor by the power of "personal magnetism."

The readers of *Every Man His Own Doctor!,* a mysterious volume issued from Newark, New Jersey, in 1875, found themselves possessors of powerful knowledge.

"Take for example," *Every Man* confidently explained, "the ordinary way in which young persons become attached to each other; in nine cases out of ten the magnetic influence of love is communicated while the parties are shaking hands. . . ."

The book went on to tell exactly how to communicate "magnetic influence."

"Take one or both of the person's hands in your own," it was explained, "gently pressing the palm till you feel the pulse beat; be particular to find this pulse, as it connects with the sympathetic cords leading direct to the heart, this being the conductor conveying the magnetism of love from your mind to the other. Then look steadily and earnestly into the eyes, instantly concentrating your mind on theirs, mentally offering your entire love and affection. . . .at the same time desiring, with evident effort of the will, that the person shall love you in return. All this can be accomplished with the velocity of thought, during the ordinary time occupied in shaking hands."

Bold fellow in straw skimmer steals a kiss on public beach from well-covered lass who fears that sun will tan her skin.

157

Summer's rapture varies with mood and opportunity. Pair above falls quiet over a book, couple at right exchanges kiss in backyard swing, and holiday twosome opposite enjoys togetherness as much as seaside view.

Finally alone.

In the Middle Ages drinking a glass of wine or other alcoholic beverage together was also a mark of spousal.

By Shakespeare's time a priest was necessary for the witnessing of such spousals as were legally recognized by the church. The church urged all betrothed couples, whether or not their spousal had been witnessed by a priest, not to prolong the interval before their wedding. In *The Christen State of Matrimonye* (1543), Miles Coverdale wrote:

"After hand-fastynge and makynge of the contracte, the church-goyng and weddyng should not be differed too longe, lest the wickedde sow hys ungracious sede in the meane season."

This was apparently no longer a very common problem in Victorian England, at least among the middle and upper classes. There is no hint, no suggestion, that in all those "lightly given matrimonial promises" there was a promise of anything else.

During the nineteenth century, the United States was closely influenced by English courtship and wedding practices, although the many immigrants from other parts of Europe continued to practice their own special customs. If the unmarried English girls were independent, the American ones were even more so.

In the 1860's, a Frenchman, Auguste Carlier, journeyed to America and made a close study of its marriage and courtship customs. He was dumbfounded by the casual independence of American women and American courtship practices in general. As Carlier was quick to note, French girls of good family had little to say in the matter of their marriages, and though English girls had more freedom, American girls had the most freedom.

In England, though neither a father's nor a mother's consent was required, a betrothed couple had to go to the local registrar and enter their names in a public book. The names were kept on display for twenty-one days and then, if there were no ob-

Brilliantined suitor of 1920's blandishes his marcelled cutie, who offers noncommittal encouragement.

jections, a certificate was granted stating that there was no public opposition to the marriage. After that, any religious ceremony was acceptable to the registrar or he could marry the couple himself.

In America, however, as Carlier was scandalized to find, there was no law compelling the publication of banns. Also, the minimum age for marriage was only fourteen for men and twelve for women and anyone who had attained these ages could marry without parental permission. (Not all Americans were free to marry as they wished, however. No slave could make a legal marriage.) Carlier also noted that American girls were quite independent and forthright, and, to his distress, they had to find

Eavesdropping on the world's private moments, contemporary candid photography frequently glimpses the warm flow of genuine feeling—in Hungary (opposite) and Brazil.

their own husbands. The result was that every contact between unmarried young men and women was colored by the "free nature" of American courtship. "And how can it be otherwise where the young girls know that they must depend upon *themselves* to find a husband."

Carlier also pointed out that certain Pilgrim virtues were no longer part of the American character. In the 1880's the *Chicago Tribune* complained that there were ten thousand homes in Chicago with daughters ignorant "of the simplest kind of household duties" and that these girls, far from being ashamed of their ignorance, seemed to show no desire to learn.

Chicago girls, it seemed, "having been brought up to do

Encircling and enclosing, love turns each partner to intense contemplation of the other —along Broadway (right) and the Seine.

nothing except appear gracefully in society, their object in life is to marry husbands who can support them in idle luxury; that this state of things has substituted for marriages founded on love and respect a market in which men have quoted money-values, and where a [poor] young man, however great his talents, has no chance of winning a wife from the charmed circle."

Courtship, in less than a hundred years, seemed to have gone full circle back to the monetary marriage market from which it sprang.

It was also in the state of Illinois that another marriage practice, long thought to be extinct, was revived: polygamy. It was in the town of Nauvoo that Joseph Smith, the founder of Mormonism, had the revelations that rationalized and initiated

the Mormon practice of polygamy. The sect thereby gained international fame and local persecution for a period of more than forty years. Brigham Young, Smith's successor as leader of the Mormons, eventually had seventeen wives; Smith probably had at least twelve.

There seems to have been a fair number of Mormon women willing to marry Smith—even though he already had a wife—when he initially received the divine revelation commanding him to wed additional wives. Smith's own wife was not impressed by the revelations and eventually the Lord himself had to direct a command to her (through Smith) to end her intransigence and "receive all those that have been given unto my servant Joseph."

Meanwhile, wealthy and willful society girls in Chicago and New York were scandalizing Americans by their marriages to

Traditions: America's automobiles (opposite) have been a setting for experimental love for half a century. Glinting diamond worn on fourth finger of left hand is public declaration of serious intent.

European nobles. The nature of these transactions was quite clear to the newspaper-reading American public—an exchange of a title for a large amount of hard-earned American money.

Americans, as a matter of fact, were both repelled and fascinated by these famous marriages. They did not approve of marriage for money, but they were flattered that any member of the English or European nobility would marry an American. So it was with mingled pride and disdain that New Yorkers read of such marriages as that of the beautiful Jennie Jerome to Lord Randolph Churchill, son of the Duke of Marlborough.

The glamorous courtships and marriages on which the American public doted were far from the realities of frontier life—and America had a frontier until the early twentieth century. In the western regions of the United States, women were scarce and wives were badly needed. Though Americans never went to the extreme lengths of the French in Canada, they did make systematic attempts to provide settlers with wives.

Sometimes, the individual western territories pleaded publicly for more women. In 1867, for instance, the *Iowa Reporter* summoned women to that state, claiming that the territory was "sixty thousand short of women to make the balance equal."

But even in western America, it is probable that men and women found time for some of the niceties of "genteel" courtship. In the 1800's, people still remembered the language of flowers that had been practiced since Elizabethan times. A bouquet was more than a simple combination of flowers; it was an explicit declaration of the giver's feelings and intentions. The signs and symbols of love were everywhere, and the Victorians reveled in them. There was even a "Language of the Finger Ring." As one American courtship book of the 1840's explained it: "If a Gentleman wants a wife, he wears a ring on the first finger of the left hand. If he is engaged, he wears it on the second finger. If married, he wears it on the third finger. If he never intends to get married, he wears it on the fourth finger. When a Lady is not engaged, she wears a hoop or diamond on her first finger. If engaged, she wears it upon the second finger. If she intends to remain a maid, she wears her ring upon her fourth finger. Thus, by a few simple tokens, the passion of love is expressed."

Today most of the special language and symbolism of love has long since died of neglect. Here and there in the world symbolism still survives. The Zulus of South Africa have for generations delivered amorous messages through the language of colored beads. The girls wear necklaces in which the color and sequence of the individual beads indicate their hopes, fortune, and personality: white for love, purity, and hope; black for marriage. An angry girl will wear red beads and a depressed or jealous girl will wear green. Pink is a very bad color and indicates poverty and despondency. Zulu suitors probably tend to avoid girls decked out in pink and green, but they must certainly be attracted to girls wearing beads of white and yellow—especially yellow, which indicates wealth in cattle.

Despite the fact that the forms and language of courtship have declined sharply in this century, men and women still want to know the feelings and thoughts of those they wish to marry. But gaining such knowledge can be a terribly frustrating and discouraging experience in our modern, fragmented society. We no longer have traditional rules of behavior for courtship or traditional futures to look forward to, and quite often we know very little about the person we intend to marry.

Into this social vacuum an old, familiar figure—the matchmaker—has appeared in new form. However, he is no longer the bewigged broker Hogarth caricatured. The newest matchmaker is a large square metallic box called a computer, and what was once considered a joke—the electronic selection of likely mates by data-processing machines—is now being taken seriously.

For a fee, a man or woman in search of a perfect mate can have his or her description scanned by computer and compared to every description of every other member of the opposite sex contained in the machine. The computer then spews forth, with presumably absolute impartiality, the names and descriptions of those most likely to find something in common with the client.

Traditional marriage brokers are suspicious of the machines. "Those computers," said one, "they make me afraid for the young ladies. They have no feelings, no love."

*Vivacity may ebb,
but "two-ness"
of couples
young and old—like
these in Sweden—has
air of permanence.*

Part III The Ceremony

eddings are important events and as such they are news. Newspapers regularly announce betrothals and weddings with solemnity and a great deal of space. This is one of the few forms of social recognition that is still sought by most people (especially parents), and newspapers all over America are subjected to pressure in varying degrees to include such recognition in their columns.

Wedding announcements, then, are more than simply news. They are also public statements of the social standing of the families being joined. They are a kind of ritual recitation. The families' illustrious ancestors (if any) are mentioned. "Miss Jones' grandfather, the late Leo Jones, was founder of the United Oil Company"; "Mr. Montgomery is descended from Elijah Montgomery, the first Lieutenant-Governor of Maine." The fathers' occupations—if prestigious—are also mentioned. Even more revealing are the places of residence of both families and the names of the schools attended by the bride and groom—two fairly accurate indicators of the families' financial standings. The name of the church where the wedding was performed, the place of the reception, and the names of the attendants are other social and financial indicators. Finally, the occupations, if any, of the bride and groom are offered as evidence that the chain of achievement and prosperity will not be broken.

Preceding pages: "Grand Street Brides," by Grace Hartigan, are mannequins modeling wedding dresses in window of bridal shop on New York's Lower East Side.

All of this information would have been of great interest to a nineteenth-century Hindu. He would have been fully appreciative of the genealogical, social, and financial information; all of it would have been important to him. But he would still have found the announcements sadly lacking in detail.

The disparity between the amount of wedding information the Hindu would want and that offered in modern American newspaper announcements reflects the gulf between the traditional society of the Orient and the future-directed western societies of today. Weddings are a clear indication of how much respect any society has for tradition. We also were once a tradition-worshiping civilization, as the Hogarth painting "The Marriage Contract" indicates (that same painting shows that the old values were even then in decline, for it ridicules the ceremony itself). The Orient, however, continued to be tradition-bound to the middle of the twentieth century and its weddings continued to be intricately ceremonial. Form was all. Every major and minor custom associated with marriage had to be meticulously observed, lest the union be doomed to barrenness and bad luck.

The weddings of our Judeo-Christian civilization have never approached the intricacy of the Oriental versions. A Hindu wedding of about a hundred and fifty years ago was something of a solemn ping-pong match in its seemingly endless reciprocities of gesture, gift, ceremony, and symbol, as though good luck had to be invoked not once or twice, but a hundred times. The family and its tradition was the foremost fact of life. To initiate the bride into a family was a solemn matter, especially since she was to be a source—perhaps the only one—of the family's progeny. And for all women their wedding was the greatest moment of their lives. An unmarried girl was an expensive financial burden, and a wife was often little more valued than a servant;

but a bride was hope and life incarnate. She was to bear children (preferably male), and everything about her wedding was centered around that hope.

To ensure a good match for his daughter and a peaceful eternity for himself, it was essential that a Hindu father observe the religious injunction of marrying his daughter off before she was ten years old. Ten was cutting it rather fine; the rewards were higher, but so were the risks. Wrote a grim Hindu sage: "He who gives a girl of eight in marriage attains heaven; the giver of a girl of nine attains a higher heaven; the giver of a girl who has attained the tenth year, but not puberty, is given a place in the highest heaven; and the giver of a mature woman is condemned to hell." His advice was not ignored.

Another consequence of child marriage was that boys and girls were married before feelings of love and physical attraction could become strong. A love-match was regarded by the Hindus, and by traditional societies in general, as an extremely poor kind of marriage.

Having decided that his daughter was ready for marriage, it was unlikely that the Hindu father would interrupt her play to tell her so. Instead, he sought out a reliable astrologer and paid him to determine an auspicious day on which to engage a Brahmin priest. This priest, after hiring a barber to accompany him, would search for a suitable husband. Paying the pair liberally with cash and betel leaves, the father underwrote the search for a youth preferably three or four years older than the girl, of at least the same caste, and of respectable family.

With good luck the Brahmin and the barber soon returned with news of a likely boy. His birth date was given to the astrologer who, for a fee, determined whether or not a match should be made. If his verdict was favorable, the Brahmin and

Turkish bride of 18th century (right) is borne to ceremony in covered litter. Family and friends of Dutch bride of same period (below) help weave traditional garlands ("palknooken") which will be worn at her wedding.

the barber—jingling more coins in their purses and chewing on new betel leaves—returned to the boy's family with a letter of proposal from the girl's father and a request for a detailed genealogical chart of the boy's family. When he received the chart, the girl's father returned one of his own family. All of the relatives of each family then sat down to a detailed examination of the other family's chart.

This was one of the crucial moments of Hindu marriage negotiation. In the caste system of Hindu India a man was born into a profession and lived all of his days in it. Every man was jealous of his degre of social elevation above the lowest caste (the "untouchables") and was determined at least to maintain it. To marry beneath one's caste was to deny one's ancestors— a terrible sin.

If the assembled relatives did agree that the proposed match was a good one, they showed their approval by rubbing the other family's genealogical chart with the dust of dried balls made of turmeric mixed with orange juice, and then they returned

English law of 18th century imposed on public weddings an unpopular tax which many couples avoided by arranging private ceremony —as in Hogarth's "Marriage of Stephen Beckingham and Mary Cox" (detail at right).

the chart. (The bride herself would be dabbed with turmeric juice in the wedding ceremony; gold was the color of good fortune and approval.)

On the happy receipt of the yellow-stained chart, the local astrologer was again sought out by the bride's father and asked (for another fee) to indicate another auspicious day. That day determined, the father sent to the groom a veritable carload of gifts. First on the list of presents was cash to the sum of at least one-tenth of the marriage settlement, or dowry. With the money, in gold and silver coin, went vessels, clothes, a hookah, white sandalwood, betel leaves, wreaths of flowers, gold and silver ornaments, and other precious gifts.

Meanwhile, the groom's family, aware that this largesse was

creaking its way toward him by oxcart, was preparing a mound of earth which they plastered with cow dung and sprinkled with powdered grain; the cow dung (which hardened to form a platform) was functional but not symbolic, whereas the reverse was true of the grain.

The mound was raised before the groom's house and the boy, clothed in his wedding garments, was enthroned on a low seat on top of it. With his relatives surrounding him, he was ready to receive the gifts. After suitable prayers, these were presented by the barber, who, with the Brahmin, placed the *tillak,* or nuptial mark, on the boy's forehead and offered prayers and congratulations.

Betel leaves and flowers were distributed and the whole assembly then retired to the house, where they performed the ceremony of the *Chumarar,* in which they held in both hands a small quantity of ground rice, with which they touched every part of the groom's body, from his feet to his forehead, giving their blessings every time they touched him.

There were then more prayers and the Brahmin and the barber were fed and dismissed; since a lavish entertainment for all of the groom's relatives was to follow, it was perhaps with some reluctance that the industrious duo left. The groom's Brahmin and barber had meanwhile inspected the bride and returned with a report.

Now that both sides were presumably happy, plans and preparations for the ceremonies and entertainments were begun with enthusiasm. In nineteenth-century Indian villages, as in sixteenth-century English villages, a wedding was a communal event. Canopies, lanterns, and flowers were carefully placed before both houses, and musicians with horns and drums began to play. From the day following the presentation of the gifts

Distraught English couple has eloped to Scottish border village of Gretna Green for marriage before obliging blacksmith. Village gave quick service to runaways until residence laws were enacted.

until the wedding day both the bride and groom were confined to their homes, where every morning and evening they were rubbed with meal, so that their skin would be soft and pliant.

The most spectacular part of such a Hindu wedding was the procession of the groom, his family, attendants, and friends to the house of the bride on the day of the ceremony. (That date had been determined by a committee of Brahmins, not an astrologer.) Dressed in a suit of brocade (or yellow cloth, if brocade were too expensive), wearing a red turban, and glittering with jewelry from head to toe, the young groom was carried on a litter (or rode on a colorfully decked-out horse) at the head of the procession. Everyone else was dressed and bejeweled to the limit of his means. Music and fireworks accompanied the march. Here the family displayed its wealth in the most ostentatious way it could.

The groom's procession was met by a procession of the bride's family, also accompanied by music and fireworks. The bride remained secluded in her home, however, though she may have heard the noise of the approaching procession with some apprehension. She knew that she was the object of all the excitement and she knew that the day was the most glorious of her life; yet she was, after all, a frightened nine-year-old awaiting a mysterious fate.

Her father, meanwhile, was placing another nuptial mark on the groom's forehead and handing him pots (literally) of money—the bride's dowry. Both processions then went together to a place near the bride's house where, in the words of a contemporary account, "a cloth, sprinkled with scented water, grains of rice and grass, is spread; the relations of the bridegroom there deposit presents and other articles they have brought with them."

The bridegroom, on a raised seat under a canopy, prepared to receive up to fifty trays of sweetmeats and sherbets, each covered with a colored cloth, from the servants of the bride's father. This was probably the part of the ceremony most to the liking of the twelve-year-old groom, but it was soon over, and the bride's Brahmin stepped forward to begin prayers.

For comedy relief the servants were then given handfuls of flowers which they threw over the whole assemblage while singing what an early nineteenth-century observer described as "satirical songs"; the songs were undoubtedly bawdy, too. Epithalamic lyrics of all ages and places usually refer in broad or subtle ways to the coming sexual union.

The bride's Brahmin resumed the solemn ritual of gift-exchanging by presenting the groom's father with money, clothing, and a vessel containing water from the holy Ganges River. This was the signal for the relatives of both families to come forward, mingle, and exchange betel leaves as tokens of satisfaction. When the relatives retired to their respective sides, it was time for the bridegroom's barber to shave the face

of the bride's father. This may have been a simple act of homage, or it may have been meant to symbolize the loss of the daughter. Then the brother of the groom took the lead of yet another procession: this one to fetch the bride herself to the wedding.

Each of these marriage processions, and those that followed, were ceremonies in themselves. They combined spectacle, significance, and noise. They were the public face of the wedding. Since comparative silence was the atmosphere of a village on most days, the occasional sound of a wedding's music, fireworks, and general din was a welcome diversion.

Hindu bride and groom appear four times in painting of 18th-century wedding. Couple is seated before sacred fire. At top, wedding garments have been tied in symbolic knot.

The groom's brother bore gifts for the bride. They might include "four pyramids, made of pulse-flower and water, in the midst of which various kinds of sweetmeats are deposited, also silver ornaments and colored garments, small baskets from five to fifty-one in number, each containing fine sweetmeats, with fruits, spices, a colored thread, rice, molasses, small red boxes, combs, vessels for holding betel-leaf and jewels." These were all received with thanks on her behalf by the father of the bride. That was by no means the end of gift-giving, though. When the bride timidly emerged from her house, the groom's brother led her to the place of the wedding—usually an open clearing or compound, rarely an interior—where she was personally presented with "a dress, some jewels, and an offering of money." The future brother-in-law then took a look at her face to make sure, presumably, that his family has not been misled as to her comeliness. Neither he, nor anyone else, could look at her again until after the wedding, when she was unveiled. Meanwhile, most of the wedding party had gathered near the bride and as this latest gift-giving was completed, they all converged again for another exchange of greetings and betel leaves.

By now it was time for another procession. The groom was conducted in great state to the door of the bride's house—he still hadn't seen her—where he left the procession and entered alone. Inside he was met by the bride's mother, holding a lighted lamp of welcome in each hand, and attended by singing women. The mother "first touches the bridegroom's forehead with each of the lamps, she then holds over his head a cup of consecrated rice and milk, and conducts him to the wedding place, sprinkling Ganges water before him as he walks; she places him on his seat and retires to the house."

Now the actual wedding ceremony could begin. It would have

Armenian bride
is conducted
to church
by elderly matrons.
Total veiling is
extreme, but
all cultures have
shrouded bride
as protection against
evil or as
sign of purity.

189

*Rustic ceremonies in
Austria (left) and Sweden have
similar elements: garlanded
bride, stalwart groom,
a cluster of friends,
a sonority of musicians,
and a chatter of children.*

been inconceivable to start it without having first performed all of the preceding rituals. They were as much a part of the wedding as the ceremony itself.

The ceremony began with both Brahmins reading from the Vedas, or sacred books. The bride was then seated next to the groom; a woman servant stood behind each of the bridal pair, possibly to comfort the nervous children. The bride's mother and her attendants made another appearance and the mother tied together the wedding garments worn by her daughter and the groom in a symbolic knot. She then led the pair by a colored thread from their seats to the center of the wedding place where a sacred fire burned. There, in the center of the circle of relatives of both families, the bride's mother gave her daughter to the groom. He, in turn, took the girl's hand in his own as a token of receiving her as his wife.

The couple were then to walk seven circles around the sacred fire, the bride walking first with her hands held behind her, clasping the hands of the groom. Each time the couple passed the groom's brother he would scatter grain over them. When the circles were completed, one of the barbers came forward and rubbed a little moistened red lead on both the bride's and groom's heads. With the application of the color, all the spectators came forward offering congratulations (and betel leaves) to each other and the new couple. More prayers were said, rosewater was distributed to all present and the central part of the wedding ceremony was over.

The counterpoint of reciprocal ritual continued, however, for several days, ending finally with the disappearance of the bride into her father's house. She remained there until old enough to bear children. Sometimes, though, even a very young bride immediately began her new life under her husband's roof.

This Hindu wedding is but one of the thousands of different kinds of marriage rituals that have been performed throughout history. It displays in detail the basic themes common to all weddings: social sanction, religious (or magic) propitiation, and the celebration of man's renewal and continuity. The dual mysteries of separation and union were also well marked and symbolized.

Social sanction is accorded, it seems, to any marriage that is made publicly, provided it does not violate any of the accepted attitudes or prohibitions of the society. The free consent of the marriage partners is not always a requirement. This is seen in the Hindu wedding. The young bride and groom were almost passive spectators of a long pageant that only now and then gave them a part to play. Even their extreme youth is significant; they were obviously well short of the age of consent or physical desire.

Even when outright coercion of one or both parties is used to accomplish a marriage, social sanction may still be accorded to the union. An instance of such indelicate force was witnessed by guests at the wedding of the Duke of Cleves to the daughter of Francis I, king of France. When the girl, wearing a gold crown and covered with jewels, balked, Francis ordered his constable to take her by the neck and push her up the aisle. This the constable did and the ceremony was performed. In the eyes of society the two were married.

But consider the case of two freely consenting people who live together in a private commitment which they consider no less binding than legal marriage; if there is no license on file and no witness to a wedding, society looks askance.

Weddings therefore are demanded by society, not by brides and grooms. If couples do want a ceremony it is because they

Lamoureux Imp. r. S.t J. de Beauvais. 22. Paris

want to appease that demand, to obtain the sanction of the society to which they belong. If they are content with grudging acceptance, they may elope and be married by a justice of the peace. To the degree that they seek society's approbation, they will add all the customary trimmings: fancy costumes, attendants, vintage champagne, guests in the hundreds, etc.

All of these wedding elements have their explanations, and almost all of them lead back to the theme of social sanction. The bride's wedding dress is a case in point. As long as marriage was regarded as the union of two families, rather than of two individuals (an attitude that has changed only in recent times), the bride was the crucial element in the marriage. Her virginity had to be unquestioned or even guaranteed, because it represented the honor of her own family and the future lineal purity of her husband's family. The wedding costume symbolized the bride's fulfillment of these requirements.

The white wedding dress is a comparatively recent fashion, dating from Victorian times when white was considered the color of "purity," and the custom, if not the meaning, is continued today. But white has meant other things to other peoples. To the Biblical Jews, for instance, it meant death and mourning.

Most brides were married in their "best" dresses or in costumes created specially for the ceremony. Often these dresses had colors or decorations of local significance, but they varied widely—as a look at the many European peasant wedding costumes will show. It is not the colors but the various symbolic "accessories" of the bride's costume—veil, brooch, crown and garland (or bouquet)—that are common to so many different kinds of weddings the world over.

The veil, common to Christian, Jewish, Moslem, and Hindu brides, has a number of purposes. It protects the bride from

French fashion journal told prospective brides of Victorian era where to get wedding gowns, ribbons and passementerie, corsets, coiffeurs, and perfume.

malicious spirits, from the "evil eye," and from the stares of curious outsiders. It also symbolizes her protected purity and serves as a kind of gift wrapping, a guarantee of newness. Sometimes, though, as in Morocco and ancient India, the veil has been used to protect others from the bride because it was thought that she had the evil eye and that her glance would be harmful to her future husband and others if seen before the purifying wedding ceremony.

Related to the veil are the "care clothes" of English, French, and Scandinavian weddings which were held over the bride and groom as they received a final blessing. The purpose of these was to protect the new couple from evil influences. Some brides wore special hats for the same reason.

The veil of the Christian ceremonies is descended from the Romans, though the bridal veil is mentioned in Genesis and veiling was a custom in the East. In ancient Rome the Vestal Virgins wore sacred veils symbolizing the constancy of their devotion to the gods. The Roman bride wore a red veil which not only protected her from evil influences, but also marked her sacrosanct new status as wife. The early Christians absorbed this Roman custom, requiring brides to wear their veils from the moment of their betrothal until the conclusion of the wedding. The veils of nuns likewise denoted the constancy of their consecration as "brides" of Christ.

The use of the veil in Christian ceremonies had become widespread by the Middle Ages. English brides of the eighteenth century—like the one in Hogarth's painting of the marriage of the Beckinghams—often did without the veil in their simple, private ceremonies. Their Victorian granddaughters were offended, however, by their grandmothers' simplicity and restored the veil to prominence.

Simple weddings of mid-century America: Sailor and demure bride (above) arrive as crusty magistrate is dining on bird and bottle. Bottom: Unveiled bride is wed at home.

The wedding brooch, worn prominently on the bride's breast, is no longer common. The Victorians thought it proclaimed maidenly innocence, and so it may have; but most often—especially in the East—it has been thought to possess a talismanic, evil-defying power. (The brooch, wedding dress, and all of the other accessories of a wedding were and are opportunities to display the wealth and taste of the bride and her family.)

The bridal crown—still commonly seen in southern European Christian ceremonies—is closely related to the bridal garland or bouquet, but it is also related to ancient magic and the veil.

From prehistoric times brides and grooms, as well as kings and queens, were crowned with precious metals and stones or sacred leaves of olive or myrtle. The crowning was a sign of victory over death and evil at a critical transitional time. (To ancient man, the structure of his society was magically ordained, and such a transitional event as a wedding was a time fraught with danger to that structure.)

Early Christian bishops banned the bridal crown as a pagan practice, but the Eastern Rite eventually restored it with a ceremony in which the bride and groom are ritually crowned. Crowns are still often worn by Catholic and Protestant brides, but their meaning is no longer religious.

The bridal garland is probably the oldest part of the wedding costume. It began as the wreath of olive or myrtle in ancient times and continues today in the form of the bridal bouquet. The symbolic meaning of the various flowers and leaves used in the garland were always of great importance, even when—as in Elizabethan times—their forms were rendered in precious metals. One nineteenth-century English clergyman wrote that the bride's garland was "typical of the gladness and dignity of wedlock, was the crown of victory accorded to her for subduing

Pages hold canopy over kneeling pair at formal French wedding (top), while discomfited bride awaits laggard Gallic groom for civil ceremony.

198

the temptation to evil that had beset her on her virtuous course from childhood to matrimony."

The Victorians, who later placed the garland firmly in the bride's hand rather than on her head, preferred orange blossoms and syringa, but brides and grooms have worn garlands of many different flowers in many forms—wreaths, chaplets, sprigs, and bouquets. Unfortunately, there was as little agreement about the meanings of flowers as there was about the meanings of colors. Saffron was once a popular garland. In Mrs. Sarah Josepha Hale's *Flora's Interpreter* (Boston, 1890), a poem is quoted in which "They shall wear / The *Bridal Saffron,* all their locks shall bloom / With garlands..." In a flower language book published about the same time as *Flora's Interpreter,* saffron is gloomily interpreted as "My happiest days are past."

Legal Proof of Marriage: Certificate of 1848 (right) bears Biblical admonitions for husband and wife. License of 1878 (opposite) attests to Illinois wedding.

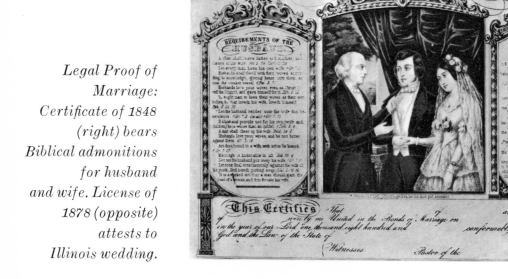

MARRIAGE LICENSE.

STATE OF ILLINOIS

THE PEOPLE OF THE STATE OF ILLINOIS.

Mercer COUNTY

To any person legally authorized to solemnize Marriage

GREETING

Marriage may be celebrated

between Mr. _Wm C. Harris_ of _Mercer Tp_
in the County of _Mercer_ and State of _Illinois_
of the age of _26_ years and
Miss _Elnora B. Houk_ of _Mercer Tp_
in the County of _Mercer_ and State of _Illinois_
of the age of _22_ years

Witness _C. C. Wordin_ County Clerk
and the seal of said County, at his Office in _Aledo_ in said
County, this _18_ day of _December_ A.D. 1878

C. C. Wordin County Clerk.

Culver, Page, Hoyne & Co. Stationers, Chicago.

In medieval times myrtle, roses, rosemary, and ears of wheat were favored as well as combinations of white and purple flowers symbolizing innocence and Christ's blood. A medieval writer observed that "the bride is crowned by the matrons with a garland of prickles, and so delivered unto her husband, that he might know he hath tied himself to a thorny pleasure."

Widows and nonvirginal brides were not permitted to wear garlands, and in the eastern church garlands were blessed. In ancient France the father of a girl with no dowry would tell suitors that "her fortune would be a garland." The garland was often the most colorful part of a simple bridal costume.

A nineteenth-century Chicago marriage-license clerk wrote of a typical "Bohemian" couple who came before him in their wedding costumes: "He, a young but well-developed man, has donned a new, black coat, the upper buttonhole of which is furnished with a rather large bouquet of white flowers interspersed with green leaves ... She is dressed in a gown of white, light material, the bridal veil reaching to the ground. A floral ornament is fastened to her hair, and will sometimes take the shape of a wreath...She is accompanied by three or four bridesmen, all spruced and with white artificial flowers in their buttonholes..."

A garland, boutonniere, or wreath of flowers is very often the only distinctly bridal part of a groom's costume. It is the bride who is indisputably the central figure of the western wedding ceremony and the badges of honor are hers.

The bride's hair might even be an important part of her costume. European brides of the seventeenth and eighteenth centuries often wore their long, unplaited hair as a kind of natural veil. A young girl's long hair was the sign of her virginity in many societies and on her wedding day it was cut short to indi-

English bride signs marriage register in vestry at conclusion of ceremony as sailor husband and wedding party look on. Painting by James Charles.

203

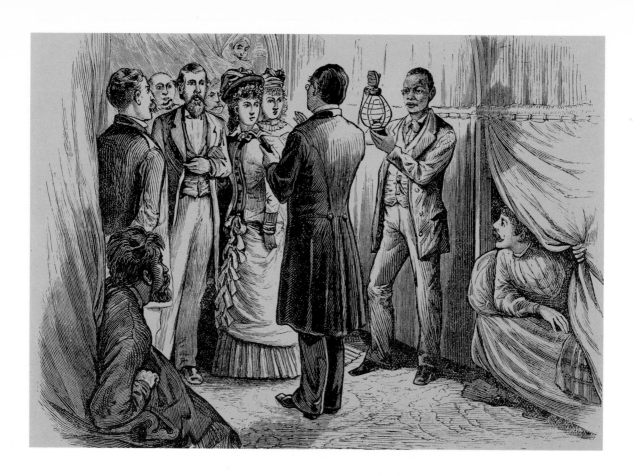

Unceremonious weddings: In aisle of Pullman car, near Harrisburg, Pa. (above), and by match-light at midnight in hotel courtyard (opposite). At right, Albany wife and Troy bookkeeper elope on skates as irate husband fires futile shot.

THE GAY NEW YORK FRENCH BALL.

NEW YORK ILLUSTRATED NEWS

The Champion Sporting Paper. ARTHUR T. LUMLEY, Editor and Proprietor.

BRIGHT THEATRICALS AND LIVE AMERICAN EVENTS.

Vol. III. No. 157.   New York, Saturday, January 24, 1891.   Price 10 Cts.

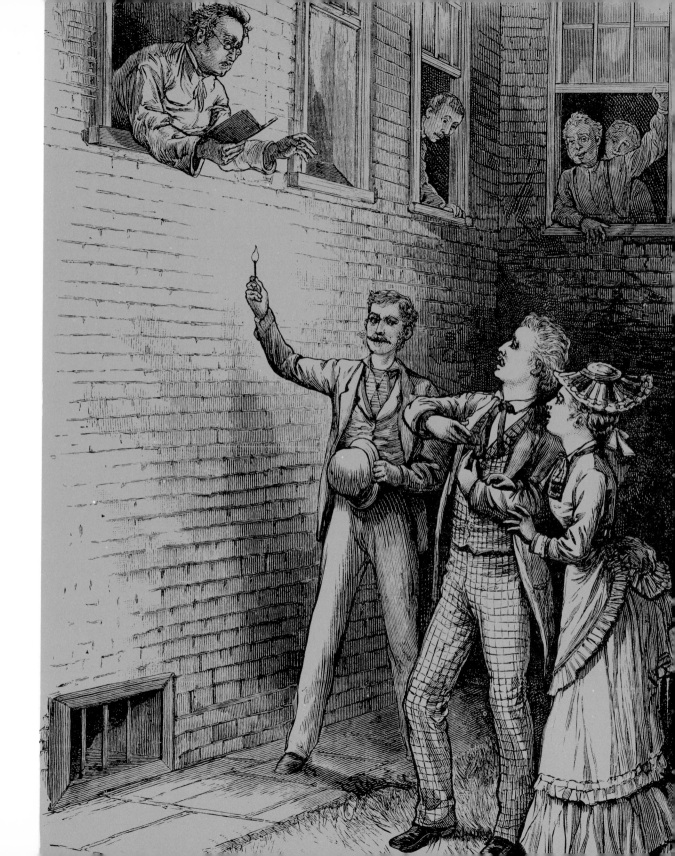

cate her marital status and, many believed, minimize her sexual attraction. Special wedding headdresses were common in Europe, Africa, and Asia, and even today a bride's "hair-do" is still of utmost importance to her.

The separation of a bride from her family by her marriage was often ritualized in wedding ceremonies. Many brides have been expected to weep publicly on the day of their wedding; not to do so would be bad form. Mock bridal capture, bridal escorts, and the "giving away," all emphasize the importance of the bride's separation from her family and transition to her new status as wife. Many European and African brides would never again wear the same kind of clothing they wore as maidens; the modes of dress for married women and unmarried girls were distinctly different.

The wedding, as a sanctioned and sanctified union, must be proclaimed. This has traditionally been accomplished by the public nature of the ceremony and by many attendant rites as well. A Japanese bride and groom drink from the same cup of tea and Jewish marriage partners from the same glass of wine. Other such rites are the wedding kiss that ends many Christian ceremonies and the joining of the bride's and groom's hands.

The new union is also proclaimed by the wedding ring, probably the most universal symbol of marriage. The Christian wedding ring, like the bridal veil, was inherited from the Romans. Originally it was often worn as a necklace pendant and was regarded as a kind of protective amulet as well as a symbol of the marriage bond. Yet, even though so much belief, superstition, and importance have been attached to the wedding ring, it has never actually been required by civil law.

There has also been little agreement as to the finger or hand on which the ring should be worn. English and American brides

wear their rings on the left hand, while European brides wear theirs on the right. The ring might be worn on either hand by a bride of the Middle Ages, as a study of contemporary paintings of the Virgin Mary shows. The fourth finger has not always been the favorite finger to bear the ring. In early eighteenth-century England, for instance, fashionable married women wore theirs on their left thumbs.

The popular early Christian belief, inherited from the Egyptians, that the fourth finger had a vein or nerve that led directly to the heart may account for the general acceptance of the fourth finger as ring bearer. The encircling of this vein by a gold ring was thought to be potent magic. A sixteenth-century Dutch physician confidently reported to his colleagues that he had revived a fainting woman by pinching the tip of her ring finger and rubbing her gold ring with saffron. As one later historian so deftly recorded the results, "the pure gold conveyed the subtle power of the saffron to the mysterious artery, whereupon the heart, sympathizing with the stimulated artery in the finger-tip, resumed its ordinary action, and the patient recovered her wits."

Gold has long been considered the proper metal for a wedding ring. In nineteenth-century Ireland, if a man was too poor to buy a gold ring, he was expected at least to rent one for the ceremony. But wedding rings have not always been of gold; silver, iron, steel, copper, brass, and leather—even sedge—rings have been worn by brides. A church-key has also been occasionally pressed into service as a temporary ring.

Silver rings were, in fact, the most common type before the nineteenth century. Martin Luther's wedding ring was silver. Wedding rings also came in all sizes, with and without precious stones. Sometimes rings would come in such popular designs

"An honorable estate":
Bedecked with the symbolism
of two thousand years of civilized
marriage, grave grooms and
pensive brides face the world in their
uniquely new roles as
husband and wife.

as two joined hands, a pair of hearts pierced by a single arrow, or a single hand holding a heart. Portraits of saints were often painted or embossed on rings; St. Margaret, the special patron of women in childbirth, was a favorite. The Elizabethan "gimmel" rings boasted poetry.

In the seventeenth and eighteenth centuries, when it became the fashion for a woman to wear several fancy rings, the wedding ring became plain—its plainness distinguished it.

As it is today, the loss of a wedding ring was always a grave event. Some married women never removed their rings, even at the expense of wearing them away. An old proverb summed up the sentiment; "As your wedding ring wears, you'll wear off your cares."

Regardless of whatever magical powers its material may have possessed, the shape of the wedding ring has always symbolized the bond of marriage. But this bond has been symbolized in many other ways. Before they adopted the ring, the brides and grooms of Teutonic northern Europe used to tie a knot or break a coin, each keeping half. In the Hindu ceremony the clothes of the bride and groom were ceremoniously tied together. The brides and grooms of the Nandi tribe in East Africa bound each other's wrists with a sprig of grass, while the Basuto of South Africa bound strips of the dewlap of a slaughtered ox around the couple's wrists. In Europe and also India the hands of the bride and groom might be tied together.

In cultures where eating has been regarded as an intimate process, the public pledge of marriage has frequently involved the sharing of a dish by the bride and groom. Here again it is the public performance of this sharing that is significant. In the almost interminable Hindu ceremony the young couple would eventually share a plate of food. The brides and grooms of ancient Greece and Rome ate pieces of the same cake. In fact, the term for the Roman patrician marriage, *confarreatio,* is derived from the public sharing of the bridal cake made of the Italian *far* grain.

The self-conscious, much-photographed sharing of a piece of wedding cake in today's weddings is a direct descendant of that Roman ceremony. In Europe even betrothals were often marked by the couple's eating together from the same dish or loaf of bread, or sharing the same spoon. There was probably a magical meaning to this sharing of food; in Sweden, at least, it was once believed that eating from the same bit of food would cause a boy and girl to fall in love with each other.

The sharing of wine or other drink is another common pledge of union. It was a custom widely practiced in Europe. The Jews made it part of their nuptial ceremony, and in Japan the exchange of wine cups nine times was the entire ceremony. Wine played a prominent role in the bridal bedchamber, too. In old China there was a kind of ritual exchange of goblets of mixed wine and honey, the goblets being tied together by a red string.

The wedding kiss, the recitation of vows, joining of hands, and the exchange of rings are ceremonies of public affirmation and commitment. They stress the bride's and groom's acceptance of their union. These are all witnessed acts—witnesses of one kind or another have almost always been considered essential to legitimize a marriage.

So much then, for the social implications of a wedding. The bride and groom have publicly accepted their new status, and society has witnessed their commitment. The favor of the gods and ancestors has been sought by prayers and sacrifices. Everyone wishes them well. It is at this point in the drama of marriage that the most bizarre—and interesting—wedding customs make

(continued on page 224)

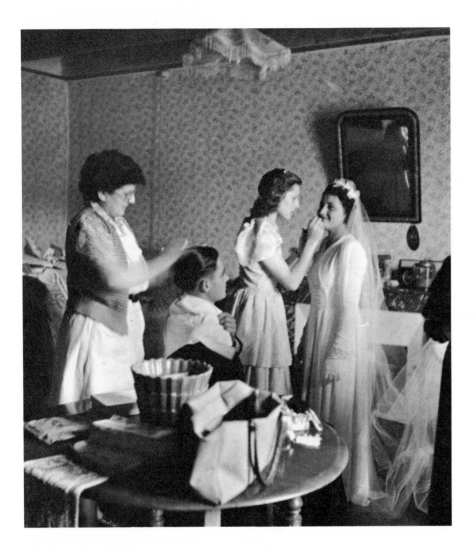

Indian bride is adorned (opposite) as
customary cutout portrait figure of deceased
grandfather watches. Above:
Finishing touches are applied to French couple
by hairdresser and matron of honor.

*Bride in final
moments at home adjusts veil
and regards self gravely
in bedroom mirror.
Right: Getting to the
church on time.*

Indian bride wearing
western-style gown
is escorted in wedding
procession by
groom's brother as
marching band
fills village street
with music.

Country wedding procession
in France. At Poitou
(right) it is traditional for village
children to block the
bridal route with white ribbon
which bride must cut.

Fashionable urban weddings: On porch of St. Peter's in rainy Rome (right); at entrance to Parisian church with uniformed attendants and lovely flower girl.

their appearance, for, just as the predictable interest of society must be appeased, so must the unpredictable occurrences of fate and fortune. All of these latter customs are related to another basic human belief, that good fortune can be caused—and bad fortune averted—by magic.

To primitive men the magical aspect of a wedding ceremony was almost certainly the most important aspect. Even the ceremonies which we have called social had important magical meaning. Wedding knots, food and drink sharing, costumes and colors, flowers and jewelry, all this symbolism seeks to impose human wishes in place of uncertain chance.

Since weddings were crucial times of transition from one definite human status to another, there was need for special vigilance against the work of evil spirits. This called for one set of rites and customs. But a wedding was also a beginning and as such a highly auspicious time to invoke good spirits. That called for another set of magical practices. The Hindu wedding was full of magical ritual. Our own weddings today are marked by magic acts of some kind. Weddings—despite automated matchmaking and psychological counseling—continue to be occasions when modern men and women discard reason for magic. We may not be sure why we tie tin cans to a bridal car, but we continue the practice.

All of the "protective" wedding customs are based on the assumption that the bride and groom are in danger of human or inhuman evil. They need to be protected or purified. The tin cans make noise and it has always been believed that loud noises can frighten away evil spirits. Guns are often fired at weddings and loud music played. In Morocco a shot was even fired in the bridal chamber. In such diverse areas as England, Germany, and North Africa wedding processions were regularly accompanied by men firing their rifles into the air along the route. Fire and lights have also been brandished to the same end.

Sometimes evil spirits were averted simply by shutting them out. In Russia all of the doors and windows of a bridal house were closely shut during the wedding.

One evil-shunning custom which is still with us is the red wedding-carpet. Just as the bridal canopy protected the couple from evil from above, the carpet was protection against spirits from the lower regions.

Bridal veils, hats, umbrellas, litters, rugs, special shoes, flowers, rushes, and other such interventions have been used to protect brides and grooms from descending or rising malice. A Chinese bride, heavily veiled, used to walk gingerly from her room to the bridal sedan in a pair of her father's shoes. Such material as sand (at seaports) and shavings (at carpenters' weddings) have been used in lieu of carpets. Shoemakers have stepped over leather parings, butchers over sheepskins, and blacksmiths over scrap iron at their weddings.

Malicious spirits, attracted by a wedding, could be fooled by disguises, too. This could be accomplished by having decoy men and women dress as the bride and groom or by the actual bride and groom exchanging costumes. This kind of ruse is apparently a very old one. It was probably the reason for the spectacle that shocked a medieval Christian visitor to Egypt. He saw a Jewish bridal procession led by a bride wearing a soldier's helmet and waving a sword. Even more disconcerting was the sight of the groom dancing along beside her in a dress. Both, of course, were disguised in the face of possible evil spirits.

In India, Africa, and Europe this purposeful masquerading went on until recent times. The methods were diverse but the reason was the same. In Estonia, for instance, the disguise was

(continued on page 236)

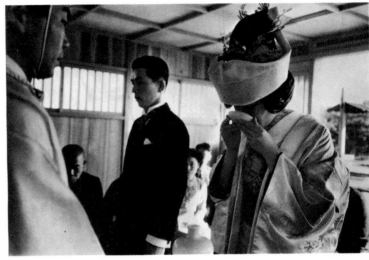

*Sicilian couple (left)
is preceded by small flower
girl and boy. Japanese
groom (above) wears western
morning clothes for Shinto
marriage with
traditionally garbed
and coifed bride. Both drink
tea from same dish.*

Above: Greek wedding is performed by priests of Orthodox church. Right: Groom's brother sprinkles ceremonial flower petals on Indian couple. Opposite, top: Israeli wedding takes place under traditional canopy held up by guns and pitchforks. Bottom: Baker's son takes a wife in civil ceremony in central France.

British pair
(above left) is married by
Church of England
clergyman. Russians above are
wed in civil rite under
the gaze of Lenin. Those
at left have chosen
ritualistic ceremony
of Russian Orthodox Church.

*"With this ring
I thee wed"—
the history
and mystical power
of marriage
are embodied in
the circlet
at this moment.*

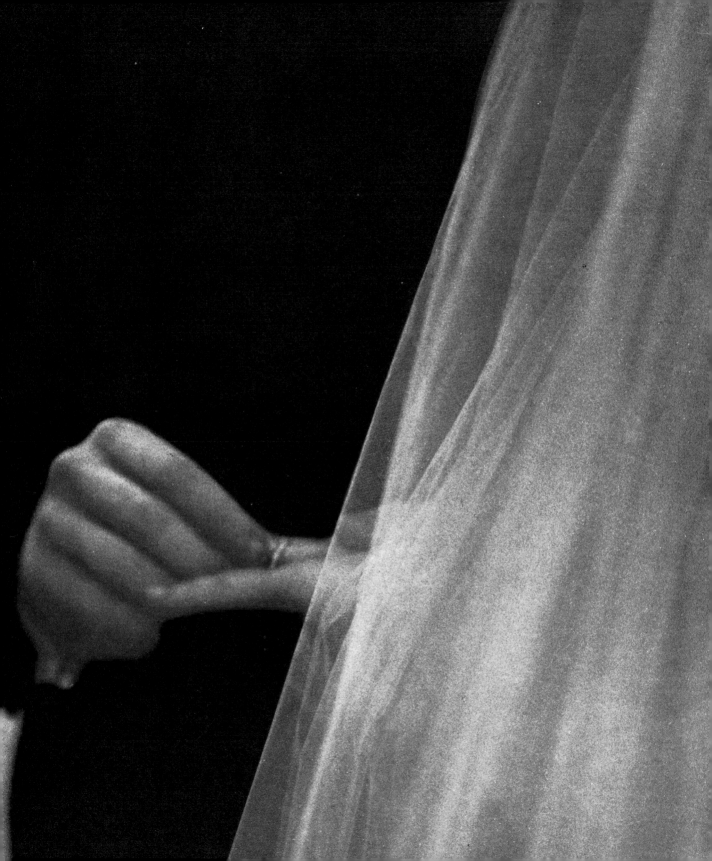

*Man and Wife:
Princess Margaret of
England (right)
leaves altar of
Westminster Abbey on
arm of Anthony
Armstrong-Jones.
Opposite: French couple
en route
to reception.*

a token one; the bride wore a man's belt and the groom wore a woman's girdle tied around his hat. The Danes were much more cautious; on their wedding day the bride and groom went to the trouble of dressing themselves in old clothes of the opposite sex and then hiding from each other for a while.

Sometimes there was a peculiar ambiguity about the disguises: in Bavaria a man with a beard would impersonate the bride, his beard jutting incongruously over a woman's dress.

In India the disguise tactic was carried to a further degree by performing decoy marriages with animals, vegetation, or inanimate objects. When, for instance, a twice-widowed man was about to marry for the third time special precautions had to be taken. It was necessary to fool the jealous and malicious spirits of the first two wives. The trick was accomplished by performing a mock wedding first to divert the spirits and then a real ceremony to legitimize the marriage. In the mock ceremony the bride was solemnly married to a water pitcher decked with men's clothing. The pitcher was then the unfortunate recipient of the dead wives' malice.

Unfriendly influences could also be shunned by the correct design or color, preferably painted on the bride and groom. The Moors of North Africa and other Moslems paint the bridal pair with henna which they consider a virtuous and protective color. The bride, being in the most danger, is painted on her hands, feet, legs, arms, face, and hair. The groom is simply colored on his hands or sometimes his feet.

The ritual bridal bath, like the ones performed with water drawn from the Kallachoran fountain of ancient Athens, has been a widespread custom. The purifying water washed the bride and groom into a state of virtue. In the British Isles the bridal bath was sometimes limited to feet-washing, while in other areas complete immersion was expected. Sometimes, as in Morocco, milk was also considered a purifying lotion.

Just as bad fortune must be chased away or washed away or simply fooled, so good fortune must be insured. The custom of throwing old shoes after the bride and groom as they leave the church or synagogue is thought to be of this kind. The old shoes could be tokens of a wished-for magical protection in the couple's journey through marriage. Whether or not this is the true explanation, we do know that the custom is meant to convey good luck and that it is a very old practice.

Another good luck wedding custom is the placing of coins in the bride's or bridegroom's shoes to insure wealth. Marching a certain number of times around a sacred fire, as the Hindu couple did, or around a potent symbol or design was also supposed to induce good fortune.

Closely connected to these luck-inducing gestures are such "purification" rites as walking around the wedding church. Although the number of required circumambulations varied from place to place, the number was always important. Evil spirits would not disappear in less than the right number of times and they might return if an extra lap were carelessly walked. This, by the way, points to an essential difference between the practice of wedding customs today and in the past. The people of earlier times believed deeply in the efficacy of their rites or rituals—*if* performed properly; otherwise fearful consequences were to be expected. Thus, wedding customs were meticulously observed, not appended as sentimental gestures or afterthoughts as they are today.

Yet, though the meaning and execution of traditional wedding customs are so little understood today, there was a time, it seems, when Americans were even less concerned about them

Groom at left gets
handshake, his bride
a kiss.
Happy youngsters
opposite congratulate
themselves, thus
briefly lightening
the atmosphere of
a city hall.

A Picture Is Forever:
Young Parisians (above) commemorate
their wedding in photographer's shop, while
New Yorkers congregate for
wedding-party portrait on church steps.

than they are now. In the bustling, pioneering United States of the middle nineteenth century Americans were often too busy or hurried to pay attention to the traditional niceties of the wedding ceremony. Or so it appeared to Auguste Carlier, fresh from tradition-respecting France. Carlier deplored the decline of traditional wedding practices and the haste and privacy with which American marriages were effected.

"Circumstances," Carlier wrote, "often unite in giving the celebration of certain unions a *bizarre* appearance. Thus it is related, that, in the State of Maine, the conductor of a railroad train, who, no doubt, was too much occupied to give a day to his marriage, invited his fiancée and a minister into a car; and, while the train was in motion, the marriage ceremony was performed. So that the man started from one station a bachelor, and arrived married at the next. It is but one of the thousand examples of life as it goes in this *fast* country."

Even Carlier could not foresee that the "bizarre" trend in weddings would culminate, in the next century, in such exhibitionist spectacles as weddings atop flagpoles, at the bottoms of swimming pools, and—perhaps the publicity would hearten Carlier—on television as commercial entertainment.

But most brides and grooms in America and elsewhere have continued to bring to their weddings all the solemn purposefulness and the joy which weddings have always evoked. Though our customs may be diluted, and though the wedding has in form become primarily a social-legal contract—usually with traditional religious vows—the element of love looms larger than ever. Today, for the first time in human history, it is love that is the impelling motive behind most weddings. Though love may not last forever, it is what now gives weddings their special meaning and special atmosphere.

Seated before wedding guests, young Egyptian bridal couple wearily wait for celebration to begin. Most eastern marriages are still arranged.

243

Part IV. The Celebration

he face of a wedding is startlingly changed after the conclusion of the ceremony. The wedding procession that quietly filed to the scene of the ceremony returns in happy and noisy disorder. Solemn, pious decorum is quickly replaced by merry abandon. For the wedding is fundamentally schizophrenic; it is at once a socio-religious sanction and a license to sensual pleasure. Marriage by its very existence places nonmarital sex outside the pale of propriety. But the main purpose of marriage—until recently—has been the use of sex for procreation. Since its beginnings, then, the wedding has been an occasion of pronounced conformity and propriety on the one hand, and of pronounced sexuality and relaxation on the other.

Times change, of course, and different societies at different times celebrate their weddings with more or less enthusiasm. No celebrants, though, have ever lost sight of the goal of marriage: the union of man and woman. The implications of this basic notion affect not only the bride and groom, but also the guests and spectators. In the late seventeenth century, when people and poets were more direct in their speech and actions, Tom Durfey wrote of a rural English wedding celebration:

Preceding pages: Serenity of married love is theme of Rembrandt's "Jewish Bride," Opposite: A royal wedding in 18th-century France was splendidly celebrated.

At Winchester was a wedding,
 The like was never seen,
'Twixt lusty Ralph of Reading
 and bonny Black Bess of the Green;
The fiddlers were crowding before,
 Each lass was as fine as a queen;
There was a hundred or more,
 For all the country came in:
Brisk Robin led Rose so fair,
 She looked like a lily o' th' vale,
And ruddy-faced Harry led Mary,
 And Roger led bounding Nell.

With Tommy came smiling Katy,
 He helped her over the stile,
And swore there was none so pretty
 In forty and forty long mile:
Kit gave a green gown to Betty,
 And lent her his hand to rise;
But Jenny was jeered by Watty
 For looking blue under the eyes:
Thus merrily chatting all,
 They passed to the bride-house along,
With Johnny and pretty-faced Nanny,
 The fairest of all the throng.

The bride came out to meet 'em
 Afraid the dinner was spoiled;
And ushered 'em in to treat 'em
 With baked and roasted and boiled:
The lads were so frolic and jolly,
 For each had his love by his side,
But Willy was melancholy,
 For he had a mind to the bride:
Then Phillip begins her health
 And turns the beer-glass on his thumb;
But Jenkin was reckoned for drinking
 The best in Christendom.

And, now they had dined, advancing
 Into the midst of the Hall,
The fiddlers struck up for dancing
 And Jeremy led the brawl;
But Margery kept a quarter,
 A lass that was proud of her pelf,
'Cause Arthur had stolen her garter,
 And swore he would tie it himself:
She struggled, and blushed, and frowned,
 And ready with anger to cry,
'Cause Arthur, with tying her garter,
 Had slipped his hand too high.

And now, for throwing the stocking,
 The bride away was led;
The bridegroom got drunk and was knocking
 For candles to light 'em to bed:
But Robin, that found him silly,
 Most friendly took him aside,
The while that his wife with Willy
 Was playing at hooper's-hide:
And now the warm game begins,
 The critical minute was come,
And chatting and billing and kissing
 Went merrily round the room.

Pert Stephen was kind to Betty,
 And blithe as a bird in the spring;
And Tommy was so to Katy,
 And married her with a rush-ring:
Sukey, that danced with the cushion,
 An hour from the room had been gone,
And Barnaby knew by her blushing
 That some other dance had been done:
And thus, of the fifty fair maids
 That came to the wedding with men,
Scarce five of the fifty was left ye
 That so did return again.

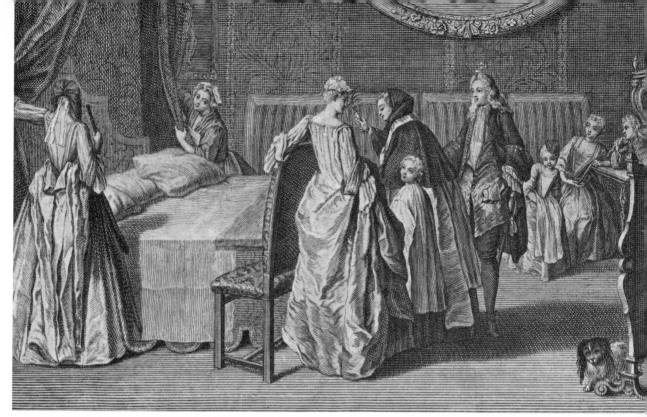

Blessing of nuptial bed in 18th-century France (above) and witnessing pair in bed.

Plumed Norwegian
bride dances
with new husband
(left) as celebration
begins. Above:
Sir David Wilkie's
"Penny Wedding"
depicts the same
scene among humble
folk in Scotland.

Not all wedding celebrations—even in Restoration England—were so abandoned. The Puritans existed side by side with the likes of Ralph of Reading, but even the Puritans, in their own fashion, made merry at a wedding feast. They danced and drank sack-posset (a potent mixture of spiced hot milk and wine or ale), their favorite catalyst for merrymaking. This was true not only of the English Puritans, but also of their seemingly dour New England cousins. They all celebrated—and set the stage for—the coming consummation of the marriage.

This celebration, this witnessing, is a ritual of great age and almost universal extent. It is as much a part of a wedding as the exchange of rings or the recital of vows. It is a time of relaxation from the tense mood of the ceremony. And it is important to remember that for most peoples throughout mankind's history, a wedding celebration has always been an event that brought excitement, extravagant eating, drinking, and dancing into their uneventful lives. Men and women celebrated not only the marriage of the bride and groom, but also their own temporary release from the drabness of day-to-day life. Almost everyone loved weddings.

The kinds of food and drink consumed, the kinds of dances danced, the different superstitions observed varied from country to country and even from town to town. Certain purposes, though, were common to almost all celebrations. They provided a chance for the two united families to get to know each other, and for the fathers of the bride and groom (or the groom himself) to show hospitality and to demonstrate their wealth and social standing. Most important, a wedding was a moment to rejoice at the eternal renewal of life that was promised by the marriage of a man and a woman. It was this last purpose that generally determined the special elements of wedding celebra-

"Three Candles": Artist Marc Chagall celebrates a wedding anniversary with romantic painting of himself and wife.

254

tions: the food and drink, the dances, songs, and rituals.

Traditionally, wedding celebrations begin with a feast at which the bride and groom are seated together in the place of honor. Before them is the wedding cake. Today this cake is usually a huge, sweet confection of many layers, topped by a decoration of some sort—a bell, tiny figures representing the bride and groom, perhaps a miniature church. The central event of the feast occurs when the bride, assisted by the groom, cuts into the cake with a silver knife and the couple eat the first piece of cake together. Cameras snap and all applaud. This ritual has a distinct meaning that goes back to our most ancient past. The sixty-pound egg and butter and sugar cake is simply the Roman wheat cake in heavy disguise. They both mean the same things: fertility and plenty. The breaking or cutting of the cake has probably always been meant to magically facilitate the breaking of the bride's maidenhead and the birth of the child. Like the throwing of wheat, rice, and seeds, this is one of the oldest and most widespread of wedding rituals. In an ancient Roman wedding ceremony the wheaten cake was broken over the bride's head. The grain that fell to the ground was eagerly picked up and eaten by the guests as an object of good luck. This breaking of "cake" over the head of the bride or groom was practiced by many European groups for the next twenty-five hundred years. (It is still done in some areas of rural Iceland and Scotland.) Our society's ceremonial cutting is only a pallid memory of this tradition.

Our large, sweet cakes are an adaptation of French pastry to English tradition. Originally, large, thin biscuits were broken over an English bride's head. By Elizabethan times these biscuits had been transformed into small, square cakes. At wedding feasts one of these cakes was squeezed through the bride's ring,

Lordly Punjabi Sikh presides over all-male wedding reception for warrior-guests, as musicians play.

255

another was usually broken over the bride's head, some were given to the poor, and those remaining were placed before the couple. If the family could afford it, the cakes might be made of almond-paste. Robert Herrick mentions one in his poem, "The Bride-Cake":

> *"This day my Julia, thou must make,*
> *For mistress bride, the wedding cake;*
> *Knead but the dow, and it will be*
> *To paste of almonds turn'd by thee;*
> *Or kiss it thou, but once or twice,*
> *And for the Bride-cake ther'l be spice."*

In the middle of the century following Elizabeth's time, the Puritan revolution occurred, King Charles I was beheaded, and the Royalists fled to France. There in exile they lived in honorable poverty, admiring—usually from the far end of the table—the rich French cuisine, especially the pastries which seemed so much tastier than the plain English variety. On their return to power in England, the Royalists did not forget to bring some of the best French chefs and pastry cooks with them. The latter quickly covered the traditional piles of small bride cakes with a thick, rich layer of white sugar paste. The confused British liked the idea but continued to break this conglomeration over the bride's head, the little cakes tumbling out. As one historian put it, "...long after the modern bridal-cake had been generally adapted throughout the country, it was in this manner torn to pieces, so that its component parts tumbled about the lady's neck and ears." This was rather untidy, so brides' mothers began to have two wedding cakes prepared—one for the table and one to be broken. Unmarried girls were quick to pick up and eat pieces of the cake, hoping to dream of their future spouses.

By the nineteenth century this English custom of breaking

Musical uproar often accompanied wedding nights or mornings-after. Opposite: Hogarth sketch of groom in nightshirt paying leader of drummers who have roused him and his bride. Above: American couple of 1885 toasts serenading musicians.

the cake had been abandoned in American weddings, but the prophetic qualities of the recipe had apparently been preserved. That helpful volume *The Lover's Companion* asserted in 1850 that "dream cake" added much to the amusement of wedding guests: "It consists of narrow strips of wedding-cake passed through the marriage ring; this, to possess sovereign virtue, must be done by the clergyman. The pieces are then enclosed in strips of paper and given to unmarried ladies, the paper having several names of the ladies' male acquaintances written upon it by the giver; she places it beneath her pillow, and if she dreams upon either of the names she may find upon the paper on opening it in the morning, and it is repeated three times successively, that one is to be her future husband."

This custom lingers on today in the small "groom's" cakes that are carefully wrapped and distributed at weddings, though usually without the names of eligible bachelors.

Wine, ale, beer, champagne, and a hundred other ceremonial potions have been drunk since time immemorial to raise the pulse at weddings. Just as wine is sometimes part of the actual marriage ritual, it is a symbolic and important ingredient of the celebration. Wedding toasts are traditionally made with wine. And it is used to bolster the spirits of the bride and groom—it often has been customary for them to have a ritual drink before adjourning to the bridal bed.

Wine accompanied by music has almost always led to dancing. Many societies have their own special dances for wedding celebrations. The bride traditionally begins the dancing, often with the best man as her first partner and then the groom. As the dances follow on, they become less formal, the music faster. One such wedding dance is the "pillow-dance" referred to in Durfey's Winchester wedding poem. It was a kind of courtship in itself, with the one dancer clutching a pillow and dancing alone around the encircling wedding guests. He or she chose a partner by stopping and placing the pillow before someone. After they danced, the second dancer was obliged to take up the pillow alone and carry on the performance.

The dance music at a modern wedding celebration may be provided by anything from a single accordion to a full-strength society orchestra. In medieval and Renaissance times, flutes, cymbals, horns, and drums, especially drums, furnished the music; by the seventeenth century string instruments had been added. European country weddings were often accompanied by bagpipes. A peculiar sound was furnished by the so-called "rough music" of old England; poor amateur musicians, lacking real instruments, played on hollow bones, cleavers, tongs, shovels, saucepan lids, kettles containing pebbles, and anything else they could strike, strum, or pound. The butchers of London's Newgate district continued to honor their newly married brethren with such rough harmonies until late in the nineteenth century. Their genteel fellow Victorians preferred military bands with more harmony if less enthusiasm.

These mock serenades dated back to the Middle Ages, if not earlier. In some areas, notably France, the "charivari" was played at all weddings. Sometimes, though, only unpopular weddings were subjected to it. The French brought the custom with them to America, where it spread from Canada and Louisiana to the South and Middle West. In the rough pioneer settlements the "shivaree," as it came to be called, was very popular and often elaborated into a ritual humiliation of the bride and groom.

In America the shivaree orchestra often consisted of such domestic items as horns, cowbells, kettles, dishpans, guns, and tin plates. Other kinds of "fun" connected with the shivaree

Health of bride is proposed at simple Irish family gathering by sailor home from the sea. Oil is work of genre painter Stanhope Forbes.

were the forcible separation of the bride and groom, tying their clothes in knots, placing live toads in the bridal bed, etc. Though some of these harassments, such as tying a cowbell under the bed or tin cans to the rear of the groom's car, were undoubtedly related to the ancient and honorable custom of frightening the devil, they were often malicious; envy is often present at weddings. Though the shivaree is still practiced—usually in mild form—in America, it is generally, and mercifully, dying out.

By the nineteenth century, weddings had become largely private affairs, especially in the cities. But until then wedding celebrations were very often public. In the ancient tradition, no royal wedding went without general jubilation, for which food and entertainment were provided, as well as fireworks, acrobats, musicians, floats, and pageants. These extravagances gradually disappeared as royalty recoiled from the effects of the

Book and dog get closer attention than forlorn wife in G.H. Boughton's "The Waning Honeymoon" (right), while tedious dinner with older husband induces sober thoughts in sultry young bride.

French Revolution. Before the Revolution a monarch was sometimes openly ridiculed if he failed to provide a wedding entertainment up to his humble subjects' expectations. In 1747, on the occasion of the dauphin's marriage to Marie Josèphe of Saxony, Louis XV of France—perhaps because of his small regard for his heir—did little to impress the people of Paris. The mayor of the city was accused of putting the celebration funds into his own pocket, but it is probable that there hadn't been much of a fund in the first place. Only five small, gilded floats were built and one, a figure of Mars, lost its head as it jolted along. A meager quantity of sausages, bread, biscuits, and oranges were thrown to the people. The Parisians were decidedly not amused and some composed derisive verses to commemorate the occasion.

The real drama of that wedding did not, however, occur in the streets of Paris. It took place in a bedroom of the great

palace of Versailles. There, seated stiffly upon his wedding bed, the terrified dauphin received a horde of curious courtiers. Beside him, quite at ease and chatting with her uncle and friends, was his bride. The royal couple was simply enacting the ancient wedding-night custom of bidding the witnesses good night from the bed upon which the marriage was to be consummated. The dauphin's ancestors had been doing this on their wedding nights for centuries, but that fact did not make the duty any easier for young Louis. Amidst the rich rococo furnishing, the glowing candles, and the jostling throng, he was miserable. Nor was he particularly enthusiastic about his bride—she was a niece of the powerful Marshal de Saxe, who had arranged the match—and, being a shy man, he was even less enthusiastic about being seen in bed by everyone. Worse still, his bride seemed to be enjoying the event. The marshal himself later described the scene that confronted the dauphin:

"When they had been put to bed by the persons of their household, the curtains were closed, and all of the court entered the chamber. Then the curtains were opened, and the king, queen, princes, princesses, and more than a hundred ladies covered with precious stones and fine raiment, proved their presence in bed. The brilliancy and profusion of these lights rendered this ceremonial all the more striking."

A sumptuous wedding breakfast at Sherry's was appropriate, if not inevitable, for stylish New Yorkers at turn of century.

At the sight of this glittering throng, the terrified dauphin pulled the bedclothes over his eyes and remained so while the witnesses stared at him in consternation and his new wife spoke to her uncle, ignoring the crowd. According to the marshal, the witnesses left the bedchamber in a rather depressed mood because "it looked like a sacrifice, and because the dauphiness had found means to interest everyone."

Painful as that public ceremony was to all concerned, it was

nonetheless valued and few kings or commoners of western Europe were exempt from it. Occasionally, one would rebel. Charles I of England, with his new bride, led the wedding party to the entrance of his nuptial chamber—and slammed the door in their startled faces. Charles and his wife then retired to the bridal bed unwitnessed, a scandalous procedure! Most brides and grooms put up with the ceremony, though, until the beginning of the nineteenth century.

Many societies, including our own, have not considered a marriage valid—no matter how elaborate the wedding ceremony— unless it was consummated. This was especially important for royal weddings. The consummation of a marriage was usually the consummation of an important alliance. And sometimes, unfortunately, it was not much more than that. Henry IV of France was quite disappointed with the appearance of his bride, Marie de Medici, of whom he had seen no more than a portrait before their marriage by proxy. Apparently the portrait had been a kindly one, for Henry, if not entranced, had been impressed with her appearance. So much so that he did not wait for her to get to Paris but surprised her by appearing suddenly in Lyons in the middle of the night eager to consummate the marriage. After much pounding on the door and shouting, he was finally admitted to the chamber of his startled bride. Henry was startled too: Marie de Medici little resembled the portrait. She was now twenty-seven and fat, and had large, expressionless eyes. Moreover, it soon became apparent that she was not affectionate, but rather obstinate. She had also received a Spanish education (i.e., none) and, being a devout Catholic, she suspected Henry, the friend of Protestants, of being a heretic. Henry resignedly and passionlessly consummated the marriage and was off in haste to Paris in the morning, leaving his bride to make the rest of the journey alone. (When Marie finally reached the capital, one of the first persons she was introduced to was Henry's mistress; both were soon pregnant.)

An even less considerate monarch was George IV who, as Prince Regent of England, spent his wedding night dead drunk on the floor of the royal bedroom.

Although the Greeks and Romans accompanied their brides and grooms as far as the door of the bridal chamber, the requirement of witnesses to the bridal bedding may have come from the Teutonic tribes of early Germany, who considered a marriage valid only if it could be proved that the bride and groom had been together under the same blanket.

Anthropologists can provide instances of public consummation in primitive societies of Africa and the Pacific. In most of these cases, the demonstration has two purposes: to provide witnesses to the consummation and, even more important, to give a public demonstration of the bride's virginity. It was always an unpleasant situation when such intended public deflorations proved to be a bit late. In countries where brides were purchased outright, a virginal condition was of prime importance. Such strongly patrilineal peoples as the Hebrews and Arabs and most Orientals felt the family line must not be contaminated by outsiders. A new bride, considered as a vessel for bearing new sons, had to be untouched. The absence of a maidenhead was grounds for divorce (if not death) among these peoples.

European groups with strong Semitic connections, like the Spanish, Sicilians, and Moors, long insisted on visible proof of a bride's virginity. In Sicily a suitably emblazoned bed sheet can still occasionally be seen proudly hung from the bedroom window of a new couple on the morning following their wedding. Among the gypsies of southern France, the *femme de*

Cakes are wedding
symbols the world over.
In Hungary
(opposite),
cake-bearing country
women are urged
on by bottle-waving
celebrant. In France,
couple ends
four-hour wedding
meal with candle-lit
almond cake.

mouchoir ("woman of the handkerchief") is still a figure of great importance at weddings. It is her duty to examine the bride and to hold up a fine white handkerchief in front of the wedding party—before the consummation. An unblemished handkerchief indicates an unblemished bride. It is confirmation of a guarantee made by the bride's father, for during the marriage negotiations he has had to promise the father of the groom that his daughter is a virgin.

Most European peoples were content simply to witness the bedding of the bride and groom; any legal problems that arose after they left the room could be settled by testimony in court. The preparations for the bedding, however, were elaborate and the event was associated with many special customs, a few of which have survived. Just as today the bridesmaids often help the bride change her clothes for her honeymoon trip, then it was their duty to undress her for the bridal bed. The groomsmen likewise undressed the groom and then both groups saw to the placing of the new couple side by side in bed, whereupon the rest of the witnesses were called in.

In England, a game called "throwing the stocking" was then played in the bridal chamber. In front of the assembled guests, the two best groomsmen, each holding one of the groom's stockings, and the two best bridesmaids, each holding one of the bride's stockings, sat on opposite sides of the bridal bed with their backs to the bride and groom in the middle. Each in turn then threw the stocking over his or her shoulder, the bridesmaids hoping to hit the groom, the groomsmen hoping to hit the bride. The misses caused laughter in the happy crowd and a "hit" was cheered. It meant that the thrower would be married soon. This was what the guests who were so rudely shut out by Charles I had come to see.

It was not enough to bed the bride and groom and sing them amorous songs. It was also considered necessary to fill them with potent drink to give them energy for the night ahead. Wine, beer, ale, special potions—whatever drink was traditional—was imbibed by the new couple as they sat in bed. "Up comes the wedding night's old friend, and humble servant, the Sack-Posset; out of an ancient custom of the English matrons, who believe that Sack will make a man lusty, and sugar will make him kind." Thus wrote Alexander Kelburn on *The Pleasures of Matrimony* in the early eighteenth century. No consummation could be assured without it. The bride was not neglected either. If she did not share the sack-posset, her bridesmaids may have served her beer and plumbuns (small cakes swimming in a bowl of spiced ale) to restore her energy after a night of dancing. And if they didn't give her energy, at least they would keep her awake.

Fully witnessed, filled with drink and glowing with expectations or blushes, the bridal pair was finally left alone. The curtains of the bed were drawn and the guests left the room. Sometimes, though, as in Slavic countries, the guests remained near the chamber making a "terrific uproar" to chase evil spirits.

The English and others believed that the new couple needed a reviving draught in the morning, too. Kelburn described the awakening of the pair by the bride's mother and midwife, who presented them with some refreshing potion. The bride and groom thankfully drank the brew and, as the mother and midwife left them, settled down in bed again to nap before breakfast. But, wrote Kelburn, "no sooner are Male and Female clasp'd together, when first come the Fiddlers and Scrape him a wicked Reveillez, the Drums Rattle, the Shaums Tone, the Trumpets Sound *Tan-ta-ra-ra-ra;* and the whole Street Rings with the Benedictions and Good Wishes of Fiddlers, Drummers, Pipers and

West Berlin wedding (above) is celebrated with zither, guitar, and glass of schnapps. French newlyweds cross cobbled street of gray Paris suburb for dinner party.

Trumpeters." It is this scene which Hogarth illustrates in his witty drawing of the "Industrious Apprentice" on his marriage morn. The groom, still in his nightshirt, is seen paying the leader of the drummers while his bride calmly sips her tea behind him. (This bridal-morning drumming was a British speciality, but many societies made it a point to awaken the new couple—ceremoniously or unceremoniously—on the first morning. So-called "dawn songs" were sung, especially in Eastern Europe. These were often ancient and are still sung in the Balkans.) The drumming, along with public bedding, was one of the wedding casualties of the eighteenth century. In the previous century, any respectable London wedding was expected to be celebrated by morning drumming. Samuel Pepys, complaining of Sir William Penn's stinginess at the marriage of his daughter Peg, wrote, "I observed today, that there was no musique in the morning to call up our new-married people, which is very mean, methinks." But by 1712, Englishmen were beginning to complain of the "musique." *The Spectator,* an influential newspaper, complained that the drumming produced sounds "inappropriate to the gentle art of love." This was an example of the new kind of thinking about weddings that gradually gained in the middle classes in the eighteenth century and later culminated in the self-conscious gentility of the Victorian wedding. Basic to the change was a new attitude toward sex. The Puritan abhorrence of physical love was beginning to make itself felt at all levels of society. It was no longer respectable to write, as John Dryden did in 1673,

> *"The virgin now to bed does go;*
> *Take care, Oh Youth, she rise not so";*

or as Kelburn did not hesitate to say: "And thus the Lovers, left alone, you may be sure that the Bridegroom is not idle.

Those Snowy Breasts which lately he scarce durst lay his little Finger on, he now grasps by whole Palms Full; he has now free Liberty to enjoy, what before his Thoughts durst scarce approach without Guilt." But even in Kelburn's time old marriage customs—especially those of the bedchamber—were dying out. Less than a century later a Victorian minister could broadly sniff at such openness, saying that "The privacy of the bedroom is an affair of modern refinement." The by-product of this change of manners was the honeymoon.

Though the honeymoon did not become widely popular in England and America until the nineteenth century, it was already a matter of controversy by 1762, when the anonymous author of *Genuine Letters to a Young Lady of Family, Figure and Fortune Previous to Her Intended Espousals* began to sound the alarm. "The honeymoon then," he wrote, "as it is vulgarly termed, being to my conception, that delicate season, wherein a propensity (to consider herself better than her husband) is apt, among ladies, to break out and shew itself most; and such prejudices, when rooted in a female breast, being of difficult removal or restraint *afterwards*. . . ." The groom is at a distinct disadvantage because he "cannot, as yet, bring himself to dispute, in a *reasonable* way, with her. Hence . . . arise misconceptions, of the *worst* sort, and longer lasting by far, than that ductility of humor . . . to which their existence is owing." The duty of avoiding those "misconceptions" was the bride's. The bride, advised the author, must hope and expect her groom to be ductile during the honeymoon, but later it was *she* who was to be complacent and ductile. Man was master, though a reasonable one, thought the author of the "genuine letters."

Some women were openly fighting the battle of the sexes as early as the seventeenth century. The next two hundred years

*Gypsy wedding
in south of France:
Bride in tiara shares roast
chicken with groom after
dance with brother-in-law.
Below and opposite:
Grandmother serving as
"la femme de mouchoir"
waves box, then shows assembled
guests its contents—the
pure handkerchief
signifying bride's virginity.
Far right: Her declaration
is greeted with spirited
Arlesian dancing.*

were to see an astounding advance in the independence of English and American women. The rise of the honeymoon was coincidental with the rise of female status. The trip gave the new couple a chance to get things started on a new footing, rather than slipping quickly into the time-honored routines (and relationship) of man and wife. It was difficult for a bride to gain special respect in a hallowed family bridal chamber. On a honeymoon she was a desired figure in unfamiliar surroundings. Not that prehoneymoon brides didn't occasionally assert themselves. In 1703, *The Levellers; a Dialogue between two young Ladies, concerning Matrimony* had saluted such a girl.

The heroine was the daughter of a clergyman. When a young parson came to her father seeking a bride, she did not refuse the offer, though the man was obviously a prig. After a bare-as-bones ceremony, the parson abruptly took his bride home and immediately set her to spinning, explaining that she must work when he did—his work being reading. The future must have looked dark to the poor girl, but by cleverly turning a tense situation into an absurd situation, she won the day and her new husband's respect. As the approving *Levellers* told the story:

"Away goes madam bride to bed, without any ceremony of eating sack-posset, or throwing the stocking; and as soon as she was in bed, in comes the parson, and to bed goes he: but, sitting up in it he bids the maid bring him the little table, a great candle, and such a book from the study, which she did, and the parson went to his reading; upon which, the bride calls to the maid: the parson asked her, 'What she wanted?' She told him, 'Something.' The maid coming, he did bid her speak to her mistress who bids her bring up the spinning wheel, and a great candle and a long candle-stick: which the maid having done, mistress bride went to whirling it about as hard as ever she could drive; at which the parson could hardly forbear bursting out into laughter, and finding that spinning and reading did not agree well together, he put out his candle, and laid him down in bed like a good husband. The next morning he told her, that he found her a wife of a suitable temper to himself, and that, for the future, she might work or play when she pleased; that he left all his temporal concerns to her management; and they lived a very happy couple together, till death parted them."

Not all domineering grooms were so easily won. In less enlightened societies they even asserted their authority in such wedding-night rituals as tapping the bride seven times on her head with the flat edge of a sword (Morocco), boxing her ears (Croatia), striking her gently with a whip (Russia), or symbolically beating her three times (Slovenia). In Russia, after being gently whipped, the bride was expected to pull off the groom's boots whereupon he tapped her on the head with one of the bootlegs to show his mastery. Sometimes, though, the bride could gain a symbolic advantage too. In Sweden she tried to sit down first in the bridal chair. In Russia she tried to pour a little brandy from her glass into his. In Morocco she threw a slipper at him when he entered the bridal chamber. More to a modern bride's taste, a new wife of Wales used to try to buy something as soon as she married, before the bridegroom could purchase anything. If she did, the old wives believed, she would be his "master for life."

Through the nineteenth century, men's attitude toward husband-wife relationships had changed little. Wives were still being enjoined to submit completely to the will of their husbands and limit their social activities to home and the closest of relatives and friends. The Victorian bride was occasionally given a clue to the disillusionment that might follow her wedding.

The Young Bride's Book, published in New York in 1845, contained a whole chapter "On the First Misunderstanding." The author warned of possible storms to come and offered a balm to disappointed brides:

> *"The kindest and the happiest pair*
> *Will find occasion to forbear*
> *And something, every day they live,*
> *To pity, and perhaps forgive."*

There was indeed a distinct possibility of disenchantment after marriage in those antiseptic days. The Victorians loved to think of proper young brides as being tender, innocent buds. As the Reverend Josiah Colton—an English divine—rhapsodized, "I know no sight more charming and touching than that of a young and timid bride, in her robes of virgin white, led up trembling to the altar."

Honoré de Balzac, echoing the *Genuine Letters* in the early years of this century, placed much of the blame for postwedding disenchantment on the honeymoon. "The expression 'honeymoon'," he wrote in *The Physiology of Marriage,* "is an anglicism; and so aptly does it depict the nuptial season, during which, fleeting as it is, life is all sweetness and rapture, that it has become current in every language. Later it is found amid a life's illusions and errors, for it is of all lies the most odious."

Balzac's disapproval did not, however, stop the detested honeymoon's increasing popularity. Other less sophisticated, more old-fashioned people than Balzac also deplored the new custom, but for another reason. In America, where such fashions at first came slowly, one Thomas Hunt could still fondly reminisce in 1845 that those "wedding days in old-fashioned times, when people did not get married and run from home, or go immediately to house-keeping, but spent some days at least among those

Public kiss is still a "seal" to modern weddings, along with ancient rituals like exchange of rings and wedding vows.

that loved and knew them, were regarded almost as days of paradise."

By the 1870's, a honeymoon was the desire of every American bride and those "days of paradise" at home were long forgotten. Affluent couples took the "grand tour" of Europe, while thousands of others headed for Niagara Falls. There was something about that damp, noisy spot that entranced newlyweds. Perhaps it was the Niagara Chamber of Commerce and the New York Central Railroad; they were the pioneers of what has by now become "the honeymoon industry" throughout the United States. Honeymooners still go to Niagara Falls and they may still return from the site with an embroidered pillow depicting the mighty waters. But Niagara has long since lost its pride of place to honeymoon hideaways in Florida, Bermuda, and even New York's Catskill Mountains. Nestled in these fabled hills, are entire resort hotels dedicated solely to the art of the honeymoon. From heart-shaped bathtubs to mood-setting music, all is directed to the honeymooners' enjoyment and inspiration. Our marriages now are happily consummated amidst alien groves, far from the family bridal bed. Should Hogarth's noisy drummers appear by some miracle of time outside the morning windows of such a honeymoon resort, their serenade would no doubt go unheeded and unheard above the joyous sounds within.

Picture Credits

The following sources appear frequently in the list below and are therefore referred to by the initials preceding their names below.

BM — British Museum
C   — Culver
FPG — Freelance Photographers Guild
L   — Library of Congress
M   — Magnum
MC — Museum of the City of New York
NG — National Gallery, London
RG — Rapho-Guillumette Pictures
VA — Victoria & Albert Museum, London
W   — Walters Art Gallery, Baltimore

Part One:

Cover photo: Peter Lacey

10-11—"Peasant Wedding" by Pieter Brueghel the Elder, private collection. Photo courtesy Christie, Manson & Woods Ltd., London. 13—"Adam and Eve with the Tree of Knowledge," BM. 16-17—"Bride" by Pieter Brueghel the Younger, William Rockhill Nelson Gallery of Art, Kansas City, Missouri. 21—"Groom" by Pieter Brueghel the Younger, William Rockhill Nelson Gallery of Art, Kansas City, Missouri. 22-23—"Peasant Wedding" by Pieter Brueghel the Elder, Kunsthistorisches Museum, Vienna. Photo Alinari. 26—"Peasants' Marriage Festival" by Pieter Brueghel the Younger, W. 31 —L. 37—Attic vase "Courting," Metropolitan Museum of Art, New York. Gift of Christos G. Bastis, 1967. 41—"Bacchus and Ariadne Crowned by Venus" by Tintoretto, Palazzo Ducale, Venice. Photo Alinari. 45—Byzantine marriage ring, W. 48-49—"Festa Nuziale," Roman frieze, Museo Vaticano, Rome. Photo Alinari. 52-53—"Aldobrandine Wedding," Roman fresco, Museo Vaticano, Rome. Photo Alinari. 59—"Henry VII" by unknown artist, National Portrait Gallery, London. 61—"Bel-Acueil Shows Lover the Rose," BM. 64 & 65—"Marriage of John I of Portugal and Philippa of Lancaster," BM. 66—"Combat of Love and Chastity," Florentine

school, NG. 67—"Golden Gate" (fragment), Studio of the Master of Moulins, NG. 69—"Marriage at Cana" by Master of the Retable of the Reyes Catolicos, National Gallery of Art, Washington, D.C., Samuel H. Kress Collection. 72 & 73—"Giovanni Arnolfini and His Bride" by Jan Van Eyck, NG. 76 (top)—"Marriage of the Virgin" by Fra Angelico, Museo di San Marco, Florence. Photo Alinari. 76 (bottom)—"Marriage of the Virgin," Sienese school, NG. 77—"Marriage of the Virgin" by Raphael, Pinacoteca, Milan. Photo Alinari. 78—"Nuptiae" by Jan Sadeler the Elder, VA. 81—"Marriage at Cana" by Giuseppe Maria Crespi, courtesy Art Institute of Chicago, Wirt D. Walker Fund. 82-83—"Wedding Feast" by Jan Steen, VA. 84-85—"Marriage of Boccaccio Adimari and Lisa Ricasoli," Galleria Dell'accademia, Florence. Photo Alinari. 86—"Wedding of Peleus and Thetis" by Peter Paul Rubens, courtesy Art Institute of Chicago, Charles H. and Mary F. S. Worcester Collection. 87—"Marriage of Henry IV and Maria de Medici" by Peter Paul Rubens, Wallace Collection, London. 90-91 (all)—Illustrations from Jost Amman, "Theater of Women," Holbein Society Reprint, Manchester, A. Brothers, 1872. 94-95—"Betrothal Ceremony" by unknown Dutch painter, private collection. Photo Glyn Davis. 96—"Sefer Minhagim," Amsterdam, 1662. 98-99 (all)—L. 102-103 (both)—"Portrait of a Man and Woman at a Casement," Workshop of Lippi, Metropolitan Museum of Art, Gift of Henry G. Marquand, 1889.

Part Two:

106-107—"Bridal Couple" by Lorenzo Lotto, Prado, Madrid. Photo Alinari. 111—Title page of *Matrimonial Magazine,* London, 1775. 112-113—"The Suitor's Visit" by Gerard Ter Borch, National Gallery of Art, Washington, D.C., Andrew Mellon Collection. 114—"Marriage Contract" by William Hogarth, NG. 115—"Il Primo Abboceamento" by Lasino, Prints Division, New York Public Library. 116—C. 117—"An Introduction. Gay Moments of Logic, Jerry, Tom and Corinthian Kate" by I. R.

and G. Cruikshank, author's collection. 120—C. 122 —"L'Accord Parfait" after Watteau, NG. 123—L. 126-127—"An Elegant Establishment for Young Ladies" by Edward Francis Burney, VA. 128—C. 131—"Choosing the Wedding Gown" by W. Mulready, VA. 133—"Courtship" and "Matrimony" by Francis Jukes, VA. 134—"First Class—The Meeting" by Abraham Solomon, City of Southampton Art Gallery. Photo by R. G. Lock. 139 (left)—Illustration from T. de Pauly (Fedor K. Pauli), "Description ethnographique des peuples de la Russie," St. Petersburg, 1862. 139 (right)—Illustration from Evert Maaskamp, "Afbeeldingen van Kleedingen," Zeden en Gewoonten in Holland, Amsterdam, 1811. 140—"Lovers' Quarrel," Currier & Ives, MC. 141— "Lovers' Reconciliation," Currier & Ives, MC. 144— C. 145—"Popping the Question," Currier & Ives, MC. 146-149 (all)—C. 151—Radio Times. 152-153, 154—C. 155—Valentine, author's collection. 156-163 (all)—C. 164—Black Star. 165—Rene Burri, M. 166 —Charles Harbutt, M. 167 & 168—Bruce Davidson, M. 169—Dennis Stock, M. 172-173—Henri Cartier-Bresson, M.

Part Three:

174-175—"Grand Street Brides" by Grace Hartigan, Whitney Museum of American Art, New York. 178 —"Marriage" by Pietro Longhi, Galleria Querini Stampalia, Venice. Photo Alinari. 179—"Preparing the Bride" by Jean Dambrun after Lebrun, VA. 180-181 (both)—L. 182-183 (both)—"Wedding of Stephen Beckingham and Mary Cox" by William Hogarth, Metropolitan Museum of Art, Marquand Fund, 1936, New York. 185—C. 187—"Wedding of Nale and Damayanti," Indian, VA. 189—L. 190— "Peasant Wedding" by Ferdinand Georg Waldmueller, Osterreichische Galerie, Vienna. 191—Nordiska Museet, Stockholm. 194—C. 197 (bottom)— Illustration from Thomas P. Hunt, "The Wedding Days of Former Times," Philadelphia, Griffith & Simon, 1845. 197 (top)—"Sailor's Wedding" by R. C. Woodville, W. 199 (both)—C. 200—Marriage certificate, Currier & Ives, MC. 201—Marriage

license, author's collection. 202—"Signing the Marriage Register" by James Charles, by permission of Bradford Corporation Libraries, Art Gallery and Museum Committee, Bradford, England. 204-207 (all)—C. 209—Radio Times. 210 (left and bottom right)—C. 210 (top right)—Nordiska Museet, Stockholm. 211 (top)—Radio Times. 211 (bottom)—C. 214—Marilyn Silverstone, M. 215—Robert Doisneau, RG. 216—Van Bucher, Photo Researchers. 217— Joan Sydlow, FPG. 218-219—Marilyn Silverstone, M. 220 & 221—Robert Doisneau, RG. 222—Wayne Miller, M.—223 & 226—Bruce Davidson, M. 227— Werner Bischof, M. 228 (left)—Rene Burri, M. 228 (right)—Marilyn Silverstone, M. 229 (top)—David Seymour, M. 229 (bottom)—Radio Times. 230 (top) —Eve Arnold, M. 230-231 (bottom)—Black Star. 231 (top)—Constantine Manos, M. 232-233—Eve Arnold, M. 234—Rene Burri, M. 235—Bruce Davidson, M. 238—John Ross, Photo Researchers. 239— Van Bucher, Photo Researchers. 240—Robert Doisneau, RG. 241—Bruce Davidson, M. 242—Elliot Erwitt, M.

Part Four:

244-245—"Jewish Bride" by Rembrandt, Rijksmuseum, Amsterdam. 247—"Ball Given at Versailles" by Chas. Nicholas Cochin the Elder, VA. 249 (both)—L. 250-251 (bottom) Nordiska Museet, Stockholm, 251 (top)—"Penny Wedding" by David Wilkie, VA. 253—"Three Candles" by Marc Chagall, courtesy DeWitt Wallace. 254—"Sikh Sardar Presiding at Wedding Reception," VA. 256 —"Marriage Morn" by William Hogarth, BM. 257 —C. 260-261—"Health of the Bride" by Stanhope Forbes, reproduced by courtesy of the Trustees of the Tate Gallery, London. 262—"Waning Honeymoon" by George Henry Boughton, W. 263—"Mariage de Convenance" by Sir William Q. Orchardson, courtesy Glasgow Art Gallery & Museum. 265 —Byron, MC. 268—Eastfoto. 269—Robert Doisneau, RG. 272—Eastfoto. 273—Robert Doisneau, RG. 276-277 (all)—Lucien Clergue. 280—J. Barry O'Rourke. 282—Brooke Elgie, FPG.

Selected Bibliography

ABRAHAMS, ISRAEL, *Jewish Life in the Middle Ages*. New York, Macmillan, 1896.

A Critical Essay Concerning Marriage By A Gentleman. London, Charles Rivington, 1724.

A Manual of the Ettiquette of Courtship By A Lady. London, Smith, Pye & James, (nd).

AMMAN, JOST, *The Theatre of Women*. Holbein Society reprint edited by Alfred Aspland. Manchester, A. Brothers, 1872.

ASHLEY, MAURICE, *The Stuarts in Love*. New York, Macmillan, 1964.

BALZAC, HONORÉ DE, *The Physiology of Marriage*. London, privately printed, 1904.

BINGHAM, D., *The Marriages of the Bourbons*. London, Chapman & Hall, 1890, 2 vols.

BOSWELL, JAMES, *The Life of Samuel Johnson, LLD*. London, 1897.

BRADDOCK, JOSEPH, *The Bridal Bed*. New York, John Day, 1961.

BRADFORD, GAMALIEL, *Elizabethan Women*. Cambridge, Houghton Mifflin, 1936.

Bundling: Its Origin, Progress, and Decline in America. Harrisburg, Aurand Press, 1928.

CAMDEN, CARROLL, *The Elizabethan Woman*. Houston, Elsevier Press, 1952.

CARLIER, AUGUSTE, *Marriage in the United States*. Boston, DeVries, Ibarra, 1867.

CARTER, C. F., ed., *The Wedding Day in Literature and Art*. New York, Dodd, Mead, 1950.

Cérémonies et coutumes religieuses de tous les peuples du monde. Amsterdam, 1728-43, 9 vols.

CHAUCER, GEOFFREY, *The Canterbury Tales, Completed in A Modern Version*. Oxford, Cooke, 1795, 3 vols.

COULTON, G. G., *Life in the Middle Ages*. London, Cambridge University Press, 1924, 4 vols.

CROSLAND, MARGARET & PATRICIA LEDWARD, *The Happy Yes*. London, Ernest Benn, 1949.

DAVIS, WILLIAM STEARNS, *Life on A Medieval Barony*. New York, Harper, 1951.

DURANT, WILL, *The Story of Civilization*, Vol. 1: *Our Oriental Heritage*. New York, Simon & Schuster, 1954.

Encyclopedia of Religion and Ethics, edited by James Hastings. New York, 1951.

FIELDING, W. J., *Strange Customs of Courtship and Marriage*. New York, 1942.

FINCK, HENRY T., *Romantic Love and Personal Beauty*. London, Macmillan, 1887.

FLACELIÈRE, ROBERT, *Daily Life in Greece at the Time of Pericles.* New York, Macmillan, 1965.

FOWLER, WILLIAM WARDE, *Social Life at Rome in the Age of Cicero.* New York, Macmillan, 1909.

FOWLER, WILLIAM W., *Woman on the American Frontier.* Hartford, S. S. Seranton, 1878.

FRAZER, JAMES GEORGE, *The New Golden Bough.* Edited and with notes and foreword by Theodore H. Gaster. Garden City, New York, Anchor Books, 1961.

FREELING, ARTHUR, *The Young Bride's Book.* New York, Wilson, 1845.

Funk & Wagnalls' Standard Dictionary of Folklore, Mythology and Legend. New York, 1949, 2 vols.

FURLONG, AGNES, *Man Proposes.* London, Methuen, 1948.

Genuine Letters to A Young Lady of Family, Figure and Fortune Previous to Her Intended Espousal. London, J. Wilkie, 1762.

GRAVES, ROBERT, *The Greek Myths.* Baltimore, Penguin Books, 1955, 2 vols.

HALE, SARA JOSEPHA, *Flora's Interpreter.* Boston, Thomas H. Webb, 1833.

D'HAUCOURT, GENEVIÈVE, *Life in the Middle Ages.* New York, Walker, 1963.

HUNT, THOMAS P., *The Wedding Days of Former Times.* Philadelphia, Griffith & Simon, 1845.

JAMES, E. O., *Marriage Customs Through the Ages.* New York, Collier Books, 1965.

JEAFFRESON, JOHN CORDY, *Brides and Bridals.* London, Hurst & Blackett, 1872, 2 vols.

JOHNSTON, HAROLD WHETSTONE, *The Private Lives of the Romans.* Chicago, Scott, Foresman, 1932.

KELBURN, ALEXANDER, *The Pleasures of Matrimony.* Dublin, (nd).

Letters & Memorials of Jane Welsh Carlyle, Prepared for Publication by Thomas Carlyle, edited by James Anthony Froude. New York, Scribner's, 1883, 2 vols.

The Levellers: A Dialogue Between Two Young Ladies, Concerning Matrimony. London, J. How, 1703.

LEYBRUN, JAMES G., *Frontier Folkways.* New Haven, Yale, 1935.

The Lover's Companion, A Hand-Book of Courtship and Marriage. Philadelphia, Geo. S. Appleton, 1850.

The Lover's Instructor. Gainsborough, H. Mozley, 1810.

Love's Garland, or, Posies for Rings, Handkerchers, and Gloves, and Such Pretty Tokens That Lovers Send Their Loves. London, 1624.

MAASKAMP, EVERT, *Afbeeldingen van kleedingen, zeden en gewonten in Holland.* Amsterdam, 1811.

MACE, DAVID AND VERA, *Marriage: East and West.* Garden City, New York, Doubleday, 1960.

MACKENZIE, COLIN, *An Account of the Marriage Ceremonies of the Hindus and Mahommedans, as Practised in the Southern Peninsula of India.* London, J. L. Cox, 1831.

The Matrimonial Magazine. London, Jan.-June, 1775.

Musa Proterva: Love Poems of the Restoration, edited by A. H. Bullen. London, privately printed, 1889.

NICCHOLES, ALEX, *A Discourse of Marriage and Wiving.* London, Leonard Beckett, 1615.

PANOFSKY, ERWIN, *Early Netherlandish Painting.* Cambridge, Harvard, 1953, 2 vols.

PAULY, T. DE, *Description ethnographique des peuples de la Russie.* St. Petersburg, 1862.

REYNOLDS, GRAHAM, *Painters of the Victorian Scene.* London, Batsford, 1953.

RICHARDSON, JOANNA, *The Disastrous Marriage.* London, 1960.

RICKERT, EDITH, *Chaucer's World.* New York, Columbia, 1948.

SALMONSON, M., *From the Marriage Licence Window.* Chicago, John Anderson, 1887.

The Poems of Sappho, translated by Edwin Marion Cox. London, Williams & Norgate, 1924.

SOUTHGATE, HENRY, *The Way to Woo and Win A Wife.* London, William P. Nimmo, 1876.

Tacitus, The Complete Works of, New York, Random House, 1942.

TREVELYAN, G. M., *Illustrated English Social History.* New York, Longmans, Green, 1949, 4 vols.

WESTERMARCK, EDWARD, *The History of Human Marriage.* New York, Allerton, 1922.

WHATELY, WILLIAM, *A Bride-Bush.* London, Thomas Man, 1619.

WOOD, EDWARD J., *The Wedding Day in All Ages and Countries.* New York, Harper, 1869.

Young Ladies' and Gentlemen's Hymeneal Instructor. New York, John Nicholson, 1847.